COUNCIL FOR ADVANCEMENT AND SUPPORT OF EDUCATION

MAJOR

Solicitation Strategies

GIFTS

By Richard E. Matheny

© **1994 by the Council for Advancement and Support of Education**

ISBN 0-89964-309-4

Printed in the United States of America.

In 1974, the American Alumni Council (founded in 1913) and the American College Public Relations Association (founded in 1917) merged to become the Council for Advancement and Support of Education (CASE).

Today, more than 2,700 colleges, universities, and independent elementary and secondary schools in the U.S., Canada, Mexico, and 25 countries belong to CASE. This makes CASE the largest nonprofit 501(c)(3) education association in terms of institutional membership. Representing the member institutions in CASE are more than 14,000 individual professionals in institutional advancement.

Nonprofit education-related organizations such as hospitals, museums, libraries, cultural or performing arts groups, public radio and television stations, or foundations established for pubic elementary and secondary schools may affiliate with CASE as Educational Associates. Commercial firms that serve the education field may affiliate as Suppliers.

CASE's mission is to develop and foster sound relationships between member educational institutions and their constituencies; to provide training programs, products, and services in the areas of alumni relations, communications, and philanthropy; and to provide a strong force for the advancement and support of education worldwide.

CASE offers books, videotapes, and focus issues of the award-winning monthly magazine, CURRENTS, to professionals in institutional advancement. The books cover topics in alumni administration, communications and marketing, fund raising, management, and student recruitment. For a copy of the catalog, write to CASE RESOURCES, Suite 400, 11 Dupont Circle, Washington, DC 20036-1261. For more information about CASE programs and services, call (202) 328-5900.

Cover design by Ann M. Williams.
Editing by Susan Hunt.

Council for Advancement and Support of Education
Suite 400, 11 Dupont Circle, Washington, DC 20036-1261

Dedicated to Phyllis Cheever Matheny, partner, friend, and wife

Contents

Section 3: Discussion of Case Studies

Foreword

One of the adages of nonprofit fund raising is that people give to vision rather than need. People give their time and their money to our institutions and organizations because they want to make a difference in the world. They want to support programs in which they believe, at institutions to which they feel a sense of commitment. Our responsibility as institutional advancement professionals, then, is not just "to get the gift." Rather it is to create or further a relationship, to forge a bond of common commitment so that we might enable donors to put their resources where their hearts and minds lead them.

CASE is privileged to be publishing *Major Gifts: Solicitation Strategies*. What author Richard E. Matheny offers us in this book is not a handbook of tips and how-to instructions—although there are plenty of how-to's and tips within these pages. Rather he presents us with a holistic way of looking at major gift fund raising that seeks to liberate the fund raiser from fears and barriers, empowering her or him to move toward the goal of enabling givers to give. As Rich says, "[F]und raisers should be aware of powerful human needs that are often important considerations in the decision to give a major gift." In a very real sense, the major gift fund raiser is a matchmaker, enabling donors to fulfill their own needs through institutional or organizational mission.

The three sections of this book, while very different in content, are unified by this common theme. In the first section, the author develops a strategic approach to major gift solicitation which comes out of his reflection on his own experience and that of the hundreds of professionals who have participated in the workshops and conference programs he has led. The second section provides opportunities for the reader to practice or polish his or her own skills at analyzing solicitation strategies in 11 case studies. The last section is an open-ended discussion of some of the possibilities and alternatives presented by the case study situations.

We hope this book will be an ongoing source of ideas and strategies for you. More important, however, we hope it will enable you to provide for your donors and yourself the deep personal satisfaction that occurs continually when institutional mission provides especially meaningful opportunities for support and commitment.

Peter McE. Buchanan
President
CASE
December 1994

Preface

"The joy of giving and receiving can never be explained, but once experienced can never be forgotten." —Rich Matheny

After serving as a teacher for more than 1,600 fund-raising professionals and volunteers and as a consultant to more than 125 colleges, universities, and other nonprofit organizations, I have concluded that the major impediment to success in major gift fund raising is the fear of what will happen when the fund raiser meets face-to-face with a prospective donor. The best way to deal with this fear is through knowledge and understanding. Thus, the major purpose of this book is to explore various strategies for major gift solicitation. Carefully planned preparation for each phase of the solicitation process will help bring about a successful outcome. Repeating the process with other prospective donors will give the fund raiser the confidence to increase his or her donor contacts, both in number and in gift level.

This book also addresses three other observations:

1. Nonprofit organizations and institutions, by and large, tend to ignore existing successful major gift organizational models. As a result, they do not allocate their limited finances and personnel in the best way to achieve maximum results. They ignore the advice of author Peter Drucker to concentrate on "result areas" and instead devote their time and attention to lower priorities that will yield little movement toward the nonprofit's accomplishment of its mission.

2. Nonprofits all too often view stewardship—those activities that occur after the gift is successfully solicited—in such narrow terms that it is excluded from the major gift solicitation process altogether. This thinking can severely restrict future gift-getting success.

3. There are strategies for major gift solicitation and stewardship that, if carefully considered, will significantly increase the probability of a successful outcome.

There are many publications that discuss, in greater depth, the organizational aspects of increasing major gift production, but in this book we will examine organizational models only to the extent that they provide a basis or framework from which successful major gift solicitation can take place. Our focus is on the major gift solicitation process itself with special attention to the face-to-face interactive communication process. While there are no infallible "right words" to secure a major gift from every donor at every time, proven preparation and solicitation strategies are available to improve your levels of comfort and success and to enable you to experience that "joy of giving and receiving [that] can never be explained" and that is such an important part of the process of philanthropy.

Overview of the book

The book consists of three sections: Section 1 presents the basic text, with Sections 2 and 3 providing study materials in the form of case studies.

Section 1. Chapters 1 and 2 provide a framework to examine your nonprofit's organizational readiness to conduct major gift solicitation. Methods and rationale for suggested staffing and attitudinal shifts are discussed. Chapters 3 and 4 deal with the fund raiser's readiness for face-to-face cultivation and solicitation of major gifts. The reader will examine many of the fears and myths regarding interpersonal communication.

Chapters 5 and 6 establish a theoretical basis and understanding of interpersonal communication in the solicitation of major gifts. A checklist reviews barriers to effective communication that can interfere with a successful major gift solicitation. Chapter 7 discusses the 10 steps to achieve success in major gift solicitation. The steps cover the process from establishing a clear statement of purpose and putting the objectives in writing to developing a list of exit responsibilities. Four exercises will enable you to test your understanding of the material.

Chapter 8 explores the various motivational factors that enter into a donor's decision to make a major gift. Chapter 9 focuses on the hardest part of the solicitation process: getting the appointment with the prospect. The eight-step process suggested here can help. The chapter concludes with advice on how to get appointments with foundations, corporations, and agents of wealth.

Chapter 10, a reference guide, suggests techniques for opening and closing a major gift meeting. Chapter 11 discusses the structure of the gift solicitation meeting. A "communication funnel" serves as a guideline to examine the flow of conversation in such a meeting. Chapter 12 deals with the topic that causes the most anxiety in the major gift process: dealing with the prospect's objections to your proposal.

Chapter 13 discusses major gift communication and stewardship through group cultivation events. This chapter takes you through a nine-step, pre-event process and a four-step, post-event process for preparing and evaluating group cultivation/stewardship events.

Chapter 14 concludes Section 1 with a review of major decision points and conclusions in the strategic approach to major gift solicitation.

Section 2. This section contains 11 case studies designed to enable you to test your knowledge by developing solicitation strategies for securing major gifts. The cases represent a variety of gift purposes and size, type of organization or institution, background of prospective donor, and background and experience of the development officer. This section will be most helpful to you if you read the case study first, answer the questions in writing, and then ask a colleague to read the case study and discuss your strategy with you. After you have done this, you are ready to proceed to Section 3 where each case is discussed.

Section 3. This section presents some of the possible solutions to the questions posed by the case study situations. The discussions do not offer specific answers, but are meant to stimulate your thinking and help you consider alternatives.

Acknowledgments

The true authors of this book are the hundreds of fellow nonprofit managers, fund raisers, and advancement professionals who have willingly subjected themselves to tests, interviews, and televised role-playing sessions. They have given invaluable feedback in the form of suggestions on successful organizational models for nonprofit development offices and modification of major gift solicitation strategies.

I am also indebted to the Council for Advancement and Support of Education (CASE) and the National Society of Fund-Raising Executives (NSFRE) for the many opportunities I have been given to speak and teach at district and international seminars and conferences. As is always the case, the teacher became the student, and I received more information than I imparted.

The impetus to write the book was provided by the Fulbright Commission, United Kingdom. While a Fellow at Bath University, England, I had the time to reflect and formulate the ideas contained in Section 1. I am deeply indebted to the Commission for their encouragement and support.

Many of the ideas regarding communication theory and process are based upon the pioneering work in effective communication by the International Right of Way Association, a professional membership organization specializing in training in real estate related subjects. The association's permission to adapt this work to the nonprofit fund development process is greatly appreciated.

J. Donald Ragsdale, professor of speech communication at Louisiana State University, provided very helpful suggestions and text on theories of interpersonal communication. He is a valued teacher, colleague, and friend.

J. Philip Helms, president of Pacific Group, a Long Beach, California, consulting firm specializing in telemarketing, helped me make the distinction between solicitation strategies for telemarketing and those for face-to-face solicitation.

Laurel Love, administrative assistant at UC Davis spent many weekends and evenings typing, correcting, redrafting, and editing the text. Her proofreading skills are unsurpassed. Any strengths of organization in this book are due to her fine work. Any shortcomings are the author's sole responsibility.

Susan Hunt, CASE editor, provided suggestions and encouragement. The clarity of explanation is improved thanks to her professional skills.

Finally, my sincere appreciation to the hundreds of volunteers/donors who have enriched my professional life with their wit, their wisdom, and their genuine desire to give meaning to their lives and the missions of the nonprofits they serve.

Richard E. Matheny
Vice Chancellor, University Relations
University of California, Davis
December 1994

Section 1:

Solicitation Strategies

Chapter 1

Organizing for Success: Step 1

One of the hallmarks of the advancement profession (also known as fund raising, development, resource development, outreach, institutional/organizational relations, and public relations) is the willingness of organizations and institutions to share information with one another. Paradoxically, the greater the degree of success, the more willing the organization is to pass on the strategies, systems, and methods that led to the positive results. Unfortunately, however, this information exchange is usually focused on such tangibles as brochures, donors, volunteers, computer programs, research materials, and donor recognition items rather than the underlying organizational structure that produced the success. We need to examine the elements of the organizational structure that must be in place prior to successful solicitation of major gifts.

Before major gift solicitation can occur to any significant degree, 10 prerequisites must exist. These are:

1. adequate staffing;
2. adequate financial resources;
3. trained personnel;
4. a history of volunteer leadership, dedication, and support;
5. a proven base of qualified donors;
6. mechanisms for upgrading donors;
7. a capacity for donor research;
8. systems to track and manage donor giving and contacts;
9. access to planned giving expertise; and
10. strategies to inform and communicate with donors.

1. Adequate staffing

Inadequate staff size is most often cited as the reason for failure to conduct an aggressive gift solicitation program. While inadequate staffing can be a valid barrier to solicitation, poorly prioritized time is more likely to be the real reason that solicitations are not being made.

If faced with a choice of completing in-office tasks, such as brochure preparation or computer list updating, or making a face-to-face solicitation, most fund raisers will indulge in what consultant Arthur Frantzreb calls "avoidance activity"—that is, they will choose in-office work over donor contact. This is especially true of people new to the profession whose desire to avoid contact with donors is understandably strong as they contemplate the uncontrollable consequences of a donor call (the donor may say, "No!"). Chapter 3 deals with recognizing and overcoming these fears, but the important point here is that successful major gift solicitation is rarely accomplished by a one-person staff.

Success in fund raising requires a full-time effort. Office tasks need to be assigned to someone else so that the fund raiser can focus on his or her primary responsibility—cultivation and solicitation. Many smaller organizations have achieved modest success with two professional and two administrative support positions. In such a situation, one professional would be assigned fund raising and the other would have responsibility for fund-raising publications, general public communication, donor relations, and stewardship support. The larger the organization or institution the greater the demands and consequently the need for additional staff.

2. Adequate financial resources

The adage, "It takes money to raise money," is not really very helpful when what you need to know is, "How much money and to achieve what result?" Staffing a major gift fund-raising effort adequately requires an initial investment of precious resources. But finding the correct level of financial support to achieve agreed-upon goals is difficult. Chapter 2 presents some data that can assist you in this decision-making process.

Publications that offer comparative guidelines enable you to estimate the level of financial support you will need to begin a major gift fund-raising effort. For example, the 1990 CASE/NACUBO study, *Expenditures in Fund Raising, Alumni Relations, and Other Constituent (Public) Relations,* compares the direct cost of fund raising in 51 colleges and universities. The study concludes that it costs between eight and 16 cents to raise a dollar, that is, eight to 16 cents must be *invested* to reach each dollar of a desired goal.

As with most guidelines, however, this one must be taken with a word of caution: Fund-raising costs vary widely for many reasons, including the purpose of the project and the methods of solicitation used. The cost of raising unrestricted annual fund gifts can vary from 25 to 70 cents per dollar raised. Building a donor base is cost-intensive and therefore comparatively expensive. But major gift fund raising (vertical fund raising) cannot take place until a base (horizontal fund raising) is in place, and donors are being upgraded over a period of time.

After your institution or organization has established a base of loyal donors, a major gift effort can begin to take place. Here you can expect costs to range from five to 20 cents per dollar raised. If you view the annual fund as a step toward major gift acquisition, then the cost of all levels of fund raising becomes more easily justifiable.

Both the Council for Advancement and Support of Education (CASE) and the National Society of Fund-Raising Executives (NSFRE) have published many useful materials that can help you estimate adequate financial support levels. Another method of determining the level of finances you will need to fund a successful major gift fund-raising effort is to investigate costs of similar organizations or institutions with similar aspirations. While no two institutions are exactly the same, you can establish parameters to narrow the range of cost estimates.

3. Trained personnel

How, exactly, do you define the criteria for training in a profession, such as fund raising, that has no agreed-upon, required body of knowledge? It isn't easy.

NSFRE has established certification and recertification standards that pre-scribe levels of training and experience for its senior members. CASE is wrestling with the question of quantifying training, but has yet to find the answer. Many colleges and universities are offering credit courses in fund raising, most notably the University of Indiana Center on Philanthropy, sponsored by the Lilly Endowment.

Despite this lack of accepted credentialing, it is reasonable to assume that a certain degree of training should occur before a person is ready to undertake major gift funding raising. Such training should, at a minimum, cover:
- fund-raising terminology;
- legal and ethical aspects of fund raising;
- planned/deferred giving basics;
- financial planning;
- interpersonal communication; and
- major gift solicitation techniques.

In addition to this list, the development officer should also have received formal as well as ongoing training about the organization or institution he or she represents.

4. A history of volunteer leadership, dedication, and support

Many organizations and institutions new to fund raising begin to plan a major gift effort on the premise that "Our need is so great and our cause so just that we will acquire volunteers and dedication as we implement our campaign." That assumption is only partially true. The campaign to acquire major gifts will draw attention to the need and will attract new supporters who are willing to give time, talent, and treasure. However, it is foolhardy to believe that any serious major gift fund raising can occur unless dedicated volunteer leadership and support are in place *prior to* planning the campaign.

Sometimes institutions and organizations that have been successful in large-scale capital campaigns overlook the role volunteers play. They begin to believe that their success is due solely to brilliant staff work. But over the long term, a staff-led campaign without meaningful volunteer involvement is doomed to failure. In addition, when philanthropy adopts profit-making business strategies, serious ethical questions arise.

5. A proven base of qualified donors

A base of support comprised of one-time donors is a weak foundation for a major gift fund drive. Donors who have been upgraded in gift level on a consistent basis have demonstrated their loyalty to and enthusiasm for the mission. These donors have "qualified" themselves to be willing and perhaps capable of considering a major gift.

The best way to test the strength of your donor rolls is to conduct a pre-campaign feasibility study. An outside consulting firm is much more likely to achieve a more comprehensive (and candid) response. The feasibility study assesses your projected campaign goal and the attitudes of the highest potential donors about the campaign itself. A feasibility study enables you to uncover—and address—specific weaknesses, thus avoiding a costly false start.

6. Mechanisms for upgrading donors

A mechanism for the continual upgrading of existing donors, at all gift levels, is an important prerequisite to a major gift campaign. Annual fund donors need to be asked to upgrade with each contact. A good rule-of-thumb for gifts under $1,000 is to ask donors to upgrade by at least two times the level of their previous gift. Successful telemarketing efforts at the annual gift level request upgrades at two-and-a-half times the most recent gift. Typically, different gift levels are given names, and donor "benefits" are increased at each succeeding level.

Named giving clubs are proven mechanisms for upgrading at levels above the annual fund category. A club differs from named donor levels in that volunteer involvement begins at the club level. Officers are elected, and members meet formally to conduct business and learn more about the organization or institution. Written and oral communication increases at a planned rate for each successive level. Additional gift clubs at higher donor levels are added as required.

A formal plan should be in place to staff and service each giving club at specific rates. This stewardship plan is *in addition to* the different tangible benefits that accompany club membership.

The overall goal of upgrading is to move each donor toward what David Dunlop, director of capital projects at Cornell University, has termed the "ultimate gift," that once-in-a-lifetime gift that greatly exceeds all of the donor's previous contributions.[1]

7. A capacity for donor research

No one area of major gift fund raising is more misunderstood and maligned than formal donor research. Some people call it "unauthorized invasion of privacy," while others consider it to be "the mandatory first step to any major gift." Both views overstate the case.

A simple test will resolve most ethical questions regarding donor research. Is the confidential information true, accurate, and of a nature that you would willingly share with the donor? Each item of recorded research should help the major gift officer to better understand the donor and accurately gauge his or her capacity and desire to donate. In an ongoing relationship with a donor, there is always the possibility of discovering information that could be damaging to him or her. Such information won't pass the above test.

While research is important, too much emphasis on formal research can result in the "paralysis of analysis." In their zeal to accumulate research background on a particular donor, the fund raisers put off any attempt at personal contact because they feel they don't yet have enough information. They develop large libraries of research data, but meanwhile face-to-face contact doesn't take place. These fund raisers are making a serious mistake because face-to-face communication is the best source of information about a donor. After every donor visit, experienced major gift officers write up a "debriefing" memo that includes whatever new information they have learned. Any contact by other people from the organization or institution also generates a memo to the research file. From time to time, the research file is updated by summarizing new information. This is the proper role of research: It should be the byproduct of personal contact and formal research sources.

Major gift fund-raising campaigns require that donor visits be sequentially scheduled. The donor who will be asked for the largest gift is asked first and so forth down to a given level of smaller gifts. This important process cannot be accomplished without an appropriate level of donor research.

8. Systems to track and manage donor giving and contacts

Every major gift effort needs a reliable system to coordinate donor giving, track solicitations, and manage competing needs within the organization or institution. Several commercially designed management-and-tracking software systems are on the market and can handle the most sophisticated needs. Many smaller nonprofit organizations have designed adequate systems to handle a less elaborate program. Whichever route you choose, the system should, at a minimum, incorporate the following data:
- donor's name and address;
- date, amount, and purpose of last gift;
- assigned solicitation;
- rating of readiness to give;
- rating of potential gift level;
- amount and purpose of current solicitation;
- date of next scheduled visit; and

• summary of current status of solicitation.

If yours is a larger organization or institution, be sure that there is a minimum level established for gifts that will be included in the system. Coordination of gifts below that level is governed by professional courtesy—that is, informal communication takes place among development officers to avoid dual solicitations to the same prospects. All gifts above that minimum level are considered to be major gifts and are coordinated within the agreed-upon policies of the system. Therefore, it is important that all parties governed by the tracking system understand and agree to this minimum. All major gift efforts need a traffic light system and a rules-of-the-road agreement in order to proceed.

9. Access to planned giving expertise

It is a myth that every major gift campaign staff *must* include a director of planned giving. It is a fact that many colleges, universities, and independent schools that have conducted capital campaigns in excess of $250 million receive up to 40 percent of their gifts as planned or tax-advantaged gifts. What *is* a must is that every major gift effort needs to have access to planned giving expertise, whether on the staff, volunteered, or contracted.

Each major gift officer should have enough training in planned giving to discuss with donors the advantages and disadvantages of various planned gift alternatives. Being able to apply this information to the particular needs of the prospective donor is also very important. Specific estate or financial planning advice need not come from the staff itself if external options are available. But in that case, it's important to remember that the donor's relationship is always with representatives of the institution or organization, not with the outside adviser. The adviser's role is narrowly defined: He or she is helping the organization or institution assist the donor. The donor should be urged to secure his or her own advisers to ensure a well-informed decision.

It is easy to "get lost in the tax code" and forget that the intent of the donor is to help your institution meet an agreed-upon important need. Providing financial aid to a needy student or providing research support to unlocking the mysteries of cancer may be the donor's motivation to make the gift. Avoidance of taxes is rarely the motivation to make the gift, but rather an important byproduct of our tax laws.

The joy of giving and the purpose of the gift can be lost in the CPA's or attorney's office. It's the job of the major gift officer to keep the process in balance and to bring this joy to the forefront.

10. Strategies to inform and communicate with donors

A strategic communication plan is essential; this plan enables you to acquaint new donors and inform long-time supporters about the mission of the organization or institution. The plan should specify the frequency and the nature of the messages as well as the overall objectives of the communication.

Without such a plan, prospects and donors are apt to become confused or resentful when they receive uncoordinated solicitations. For example, a local church had conducted a fall campaign for financial support. Five months later it was holding a spring phonathon focusing on the needs of the town's plasma center. But when a volunteer called a potential donor, the prospect laughed and said, "The only time I hear from you is when you need blood or money." A communication plan would have helped avoid this type of response.

Don't assume that potential donors will understand your institution's "case" (its compelling statement of its need for support) if they have only seen it in one communication piece. One reading is not usually enough to enable donors to make the connection between their philanthropic desires and the mission of the institution. Instead, present messages that support one another and that arrive in logical sequence and with sufficient frequency. In this way the donor will begin to understand the institution's needs and to consider his or her own priorities.

Before you begin to plan for a major gift fund-raising effort, review each of these 10 prerequisites and apply them to the situation of your institution. Some elements have more relevance to specific goals and objectives than others. Like snowflakes, no organization or institution is *exactly* like another. Nevertheless, the experience of nonprofits that have been successful in raising major gifts points to these 10 elements as important to any fund-raising effort.

Note

[1] David R. Dunlop, "Strategic Management of a Major Gift Program," in Roy Muir and Jerry May, ed., *Developing an Effective Major Gift Program: From Managing Staff to Soliciting Gifts* (Washington, DC: Council for Advancement and Support of Education, 1993), 7.

Chapter 2

Lessons from the Literature and Conventional Wisdom

S uppose you were given the task of organizing an office to carry out the full range of external outreach for a medium-sized nonprofit organization. Activities should, at a minimum, include development, communications, and administrative services. Money is limited, but fortunately the board of directors is willing to invest sufficient funds if you can give them some reasonable assurance of success. The board also requires some data to support each of your recommendations.

Your short-term goals are to immediately begin an aggressive annual fund telemarketing program, to upgrade donors through the use of giving clubs, and to develop a comprehensive communication strategy. The longer-term goal is to conduct a feasibility study and commence a major gift campaign within five years.

Where do you start? What data will prove the most helpful? Are the short-term and long-term goals compatible?

The literature

Since your nonprofit organization has no fund-raising history, you decide to look at the philanthropic patterns of donors to other organizations and institutions. A review of available reports yields the following information:

1. Individuals are the source of over 90 percent of all contributions. According to *Giving U.S.A.,* individuals gave 81.9 percent outright, 6.6 percent as bequests, and 2.0 percent as matching corporate gifts.[1]

Conclusion: In the beginning, you should allocate resources and personnel to contact and communicate with individuals rather than foundations and corporations.

2. Total philanthropy has grown more than 40 percent in the past 20 years. Total giving in 1970 was $88.3 billion. By 1992, giving increased to $124.3

billion. Giving has increased annually 24 times since 1962.[2]

Conclusion: Philanthropy is big business! It seems safe to assume that the giving pie will continue to grow in the future, and that the pie will not be sliced thinner; private support will provide a larger portion of your total resource needs. A major investment in outreach activities seems wise.

3. Individual gains are eroded by inflation. In 1992, "total giving increased about 6.4 percent, which amounts to a 2.3 percent increase when adjusted for inflation."[3] For the higher education sector, private contributions now cover a slightly smaller share of current dollar institutional expenditures.

Conclusion: You need to develop a strategy to upgrade annual fund donors at a rate higher than current inflation. Each donor should be asked each year to give a gift that produces a post-inflation net dollar increase. Annual operating cost increases must be kept below reasonable projections of the rate of increases of gift income. Staff and supporting expenditures will be added based on the ability of the organization/institution to outproduce projected budgetary increases.

4. "The incidence of volunteering has a direct relationship to the amount of contributions. The percentage of income contributed increases directly with the number of hours volunteered," according to "Giving and Volunteering in the United States," a survey conducted by Independent Sector in 1988.[4] Finally some hard data have been produced that lend weight to the conventional wisdom that volunteering and giving are interdependent.

Conclusion: You need to develop strategies to create volunteer opportunities for a broad segment of your donor base. These volunteers must be stewarded at as high a level as possible. An ongoing stewardship program to thank volunteers and donors is essential.

5. "Among the most frequently mentioned reasons for giving to charities were that they (a) served a worthy cause; (b) helped the poor and needy; and (c) did good work or had high-quality programs," according to "Giving and Volunteering in the United States."[5]

Conclusion: Volunteers and donors think about the reasons for their support. A communication plan must take these reasons into account and reinforce the importance of the nonprofit's mission. Volunteers should be asked what made them decide to give of their most valuable asset—themselves. Similarly, donors should be asked to say why they have provided financial support. These reasons may suggest a strategy that will lead to even higher levels of volunteering and giving.

6. A slight minority of people (45 percent) think that "charities generally spend their funds wisely."[6]

Conclusion: Donors need to hear about how their gifts are spent. The administrative services office must be staffed to provide prompt and comprehensive gift reports. Donors should receive personal reports on the use of their gifts. Volunteer boards with staff guidance must make wise decisions about the use and priority of private donations.

7. "Gifts under $5,000 provided larger total amounts than did gifts of $5,000 and over.... Although gifts of $5,000 and over constituted but a fraction of the number of gifts (0.5 percent), they accounted for 44.3 percent of all the monies received...."[7] This finding applies to higher education, but it has broad general application for other nonprofit institutions and organizations.

Conclusion: You need to have parallel activities moving forward at the same time. An aggressive, broad-based annual fund effort needs to be in operation to build a foundation of donors. This activity will yield more than 90 percent of the number of gifts received, but just over 50 percent of the value of all gifts received.

Simultaneously, a gift-upgrading program should be moving donors into the major gift levels (whatever that level is for your organization or institution). You also need to establish an intensive donor contact strategy. In order to accomplish these activities, personnel will be needed for the annual fund program, and major gift officers will be required to carry out the donor cultivation.

Allocate resources toward potential results. Both annual fund donor base-building and upgraded major gift solicitation are important. However, major gift activity should yield more gifts per dollars spent on personnel by at least a factor of five.

As the nonprofit organization moves toward a major gift campaign, the percentage of gifts from the annual fund will gradually reflect less of the increasing total private support. Universities with a 10-year history of major gift efforts commonly find that 95 percent of their gift total comes from 5 percent or less of their donor base.

The conventional wisdom

Your review of the data above should give you helpful suggestions on how to allocate resources and personnel at your nonprofit. But while you have been reading reports and surveys, you have also been interviewing heads of nonprofits similar to your own. It seems that you hear the same things over and over. The most commonly repeated conventional wisdom is summarized below.

1. People give to people. Not to organizations, not to institutions, not to positions (but see the discussion below, "People Give to Peers")—people give to other people. "Nearly seven out of 10 people agreed that being asked by someone they knew well was the form of solicitation that was more or most likely to result in a donation," according to "Giving and Volunteering in the United States."[8] Donors prefer to meet the people who are making things happen and producing results in the organization or institution. They want to hear firsthand how a scientific breakthrough was discovered or how a symphony was scored.

Neither the high rank, the long history, nor the compelling need will eliminate the donors' longing to "touch their philanthropy."

Conclusion: Major gifts will not result from phone calls, letters, or written proposals alone. Trained personnel must be hired to solicit major gifts personally. Other people within the nonprofit organization must be prepared to participate actively in the solicitation process. A higher yield of gifts will result if a personal relationship is developed. Sufficient personnel must be hired to conduct this cultivation.

2. People give to peers. Peer gauging is an inseparable part of the major gift process. Try to determine which volunteers or donors consider themselves to be peers of which prospects and then verify that judgment from other sources. Ask other volunteers to review the accuracy of your conclusions. For each major donor prospect, you should be able to select a peer from within the institution or organization or from the volunteer leadership. These pairings form the potential calling team.

Conclusion: Select volunteer leadership not only on the basis of their ability to give time and money, but also on the basis of their ability to help secure gifts from peers. To do this you will need both formal and informal research. Personnel must be hired to provide staff research support.

3. People give to vision rather than to need. According to Larry Wilson of Wilson Learning Associates in Minneapolis, the majority of people who volunteer do so in order to provide meaning to their life. Volunteers want to reach beyond themselves to help others, to "make the world a better place." Many nonprofits ignore this fact and concentrate on the importance of their needs rather than the needs of the volunteer or donor.

Charles Schulz provides an excellent example when he draws Linus standing in the middle of the pumpkin patch on Halloween waiting for the Great Pumpkin to appear. Linus is steadfast in anticipating a positive outcome on the basis of his need. Unfortunately, need will not produce either the Great Pumpkin or a major gift to your institution.

The success of the slogan of the United Negro College Fund, "A mind is a terrible thing to waste," is the result of the Fund's attention to the vision rather than the need of America's historically black colleges and universities.

Conclusion: A vision that meets the donor's need must be developed and communicated convincingly on an ongoing basis. This task requires a talented communications staff with sufficient resources to develop a promotional communications strategy.

4. Donors decide. As nonprofit staffs become better trained, they tend to dictate philanthropic objectives to their support base. The thinking is stated as follows: "Our priority needs match your giving objectives." This is a dangerous assumption.

Donors demonstrate again and again that they will evaluate the information presented and then make the decision whether or not to support a given need. Take the case of the United States' corporate sector. According to *Voluntary Support of Education,* "Over the past thirty years the public-institution share (higher education) of corporate support has risen steadily from less than 25 percent to 50 percent."[9] The corporate sector has developed a solid research linkage with public colleges and universities that has proven mutually beneficial to both parties.

During the past few years, however, corporations have become concerned about the precollege education of "tomorrow's work force." Concern over lack of global competitiveness is a major factor in the shift of corporate philanthropy to this problem area. Corporations still support higher education at increasing levels. Support has more than doubled since 1970.

Conclusion: It would be wise to monitor donor attitudes, both of individuals and of foundations and corporations, to see if any shifts are taking place that would affect your institution or organization. Are your priorities in line with your donor's priorities? Is a reevaluation warranted?

Carefully review the above data and conventional wisdom. Does an organizational pattern begin to emerge that dictates the allocation of resources and personnel? Can you develop a plan that maximizes each dollar invested?

Notes

[1] *Giving U.S.A.* (New York: AAFRC Trust for Philanthropy, 1993), 10.

[2] Ibid., 20-21.

[3] Ibid., 24.

[4] "Giving and Volunteering in the United States" (Washington, DC: Independent Sector, 1988), 2.

[5] Ibid.

[6] Ibid., 59.

[7] *Voluntary Support of Education,* 1988-89 (New York: Council for Aid to Education), 11.

[8] "Giving and Volunteering," 2.

[9] *Voluntary Support.*

Chapter 3

Conducting a Personal Communication Inventory

W e've discussed what your institution needs to do to prepare for major gift solicitation, but now the focus is on you. How do *you* need to prepare for a donor-cultivation visit? The first step is to assess your communication skills and deficiencies. This exercise focuses on a personal inventory of your readiness to communicate effectively with a prospective donor. It is not necessary to have a set of communication standards (there are none) against which to measure your abilities. This inventory is your personal opinion of your skills and deficiencies. You can use the assessments of others (friends and colleagues) as a check against your own view, but that will come later.

Fears as barriers to effective communication

Begin your assessment by making a list of the fears that hinder your ability to have effective one-on-one communication. Be honest with yourself here, and list your fears in descending order of importance. When you have finished, compare your list with the one below, and you will see that you are not alone. No doubt you will find that your fears are shared by many in the profession.

Fear of failure. Put 100 advancement professionals in a room and ask them, "What is your greatest fear regarding interpersonal communication?" The majority will quickly reply "fear of failure to achieve the objective." When asked what their objective is, the majority will say they are not sure. Ultimately, the objective is to secure a major gift for the institution or organization, but many intermediate objectives must be accomplished.

When asked, these same people who express failure as their greatest fear can rarely pinpoint a past failure that resulted in an extremely negative outcome. They can remember being turned down for a gift or receiving a much smaller gift than anticipated, but most advancement officers realize that these situations are a normal part of the solicitation process.

If you placed "fear of failure" high on your list, try to recall past communication situations that you deemed failures. What were the circumstances? Did the communication terminate the relationship? Was it an unpleasant experience?

According to *Giving U.S.A.*, donors "who are asked to contribute give more and give more often."[1] To be successful we must ask people to give. Occasionally we fail (the donor says "no"). But our only alternatives are not to ask or to accept occasional failure as part of our job. Nevertheless, even this expectation of occasional failure can be substantially reduced by following the step-by-step preparation process described in later chapters.

Fear of rejection. Often the people who say that they fear rejection are those who take every rejection personally: "The prospect who rejects my project rejects me!" "My proposal is rejected because of the prospect's negative feelings toward me as a person!"

This fear is based on the major gift officer's failure to separate himself or herself from what is being proposed. To avoid doing this, remember that you are a professional carrying out your responsibilities. The prospect's decision to support or to reject the proposal will be made on the merits of the proposal, not on your qualities as a person.

If you can separate your own self-image from the proposal, you will be able to listen to the prospect's response. And even if this response results in rejection of the particular proposal, the rejection is not necessarily the end of the matter, as you will see in Chapter 12. The rejected proposal can serve as the outline for the next one, which speaks more directly to the donor's interests.

Fear of lack of knowledge. Advancement officers often say that they are afraid the prospect will ask a question that "I can't answer." If you have this fear, you may find yourself postponing contact with the donor until you have *all* the information. But when will that be? You will quickly realize that you will *never* have all the facts regarding a project, and you'll just have to go ahead without them. But this does not mean that you should not thoroughly prepare yourself before making a donor solicitation. Preparation is one of a professional's most important tools. The line between being adequately prepared and knowing it all is a fine one, but the distinction is important.

A second reaction to this fear is to prepare for the conversation by rehearsing both sides. "I'll open with ... then she will say ... then I'll respond... etc." This approach can lead to disastrous consequences, the greatest of which is failure to listen. The donor's inevitable failure to "follow the script" usually leads to panic or, sometimes, annoyance that the donor is not cooperating with the prearranged scenario. But this fear always disappears when you look at the possible consequences of a lack of knowledge. Suppose you are the officer in the following conversation:

> **Donor:** The return on your endowment funds seems high. How does it compare with that of other institutions?

> **Officer:** I believe the returns are quite good. I've seen comparative figures but I can't recall them. I'll get that information and get back to you.

Donor: Thank you very much. I'd appreciate it. Give me a call when you have the information.

Your fear has come true, and the donor has asked you something you don't know. But consider the consequences of your failure to know the requested information:

1. You established credibility with this donor by making it clear that you will only answer his concerns with information about which you are confident.

2. You assured the donor that his concerns are important and should be validated.

3. You displayed responsibility by promising specific follow-up. (Be sure to carry through or trust will be eroded.)

4. You established the basis for a follow-up call.

Not a bad outcome for a sometimes-paralyzing fear!

Fear of loss of control. Entering into a conversation where the goal is to seek information and develop rapport can be frightening. The outcome is not predictable. Success is not guaranteed. You are *not* in control.

Development officers who have this fear normally fight it by learning a "pitch" about their organization or institution. It is as though a telemarketing script governed the conversation. Talking means control. Listening may lead to new discoveries, and control is transferred to the donor.

The four myths of major gift solicitation are discussed in Chapter 4. These myths have great relevance to this fear. After reading Chapter 4, come back and reread these comments about fear of loss of control. And remember that both the speaker and the listener in a conversation, like the driver and the passenger in a car, usually arrive at the same place at the same time—if both parties agree on the route and the destination.

Qualities and abilities for effective communication

Now that we have covered the fears that can decrease your ability to communicate, let's examine the personal qualities and abilities that can make you more effective in face-to-face communication. Ask the same 100 advancement professionals to list the qualities that make them effective communicators, and they will likely mention the following:

Enthusiasm for the mission. If you enthusiastically embrace the mission of the organization or institution you represent, you have already taken the first and most important step toward success. You want to share your enthusiasm. You want others to feel as you do. You are proud of the "product." Your positive energy will show and will be readily communicated to the donor if you have listened well enough to understand how he or she is likely to think and respond.

Downside? You may talk too much and therefore listen too little. But by also becoming an enthusiastic listener, you will create an unbeatable combination.

Caring about people. Concern for others is a basic ingredient of success in major gift fund raising. This concern is an important building block in establishing a long-term relationship. People who claim this as a strength see themselves as serving the needs of donors and helping them achieve their philanthropic goals and objectives. This attitude of being in "one of the helping professions" is an important asset in building trust with donors.

Attitude is a basic ingredient in communication.[2] If you believe that your nonprofit's mission is critical to the well-being of society, you will be enthusiastic about involving the donor in this mission. If you care about people, you want to be with people. This makes face-to-face contact a positive experience. If this is your attitude, you will be unlikely—or at least less likely—to delay making contact with your major donor prospects.

Ability to be a good listener. Volumes of excellent material are available on listening skills and monitoring of nonverbal clues. How important these parts of communication are is brought home when we learn that studies show that listening is more than 50 percent of communication, and monitoring nonverbal clues affects over 90 percent of the message. You may wish to review some of the available material on communications to sensitize yourself to the importance of listening.

Is it enough to "pay attention" to the donor? Is "paying attention" the same as listening? Aren't both activities passive in nature? The answer to all three questions is "no." Listening is a willful act. When you do "aggressive listening," you purposely focus on the act of hearing and "seeing the conversation" from the donor's point of view. Research tells us that, during a conversation, an aggressive listener has a more rapid pulse rate than a passive listener. Palms may become sweaty. This listener is exercising his or her skills in information-seeking.

Have you ever discovered different levels of listening ability as you debrief with another development officer after meeting with a prospective donor? One person gathered a lot of relevant information, including requests by the donor for follow-up areas and clues for further exploration. The other person heard very little and saw less. Is one of these people not listening? No, both are listening, but one has learned to listen aggressively and values the skill. The non-listener has yet to relate listening to positive outcomes.

Listening is a compliment to the speaker. Active listening in a crowd with full attention on the speaker is a rare skill practiced by few. Whether you are one-on-one or one-of-a-hundred, listen to donors. They are giving you a valuable gift—their opinions.

The attributes listed in this chapter are those most often cited by major gift development officers as helping them communicate successfully. What are yours? How do yours measure up? Later chapters will help you work on developing your communication abilities.

Notes

[1] *Giving U.S.A.* (New York: AAFRC Trust for Philanthropy, 1993), 51.

[2] David K. Berlo, *The Process of Communication* (New York: Holt, Rinehart and Winston, 1960), 72.

Chapter 4

Myths Regarding Major Gift Solicitation

Over the years, the advancement profession has adopted certain myths about major gift solicitation. The myths probably arose as rationalizations for avoiding face-to-face contact with donors. Rarely are the myths written down or discussed because they would not stand up under closer examination. Nevertheless, they can and do exert a powerful influence on many major gift officers. They are:

1. "Most people are too busy and are not interested in being friendly with me."
2. "Most people do not like to talk about themselves."
3. "People will reject personal support and attention."
4. "If I could learn 'the right words to say,' then I would be more successful in calling on major gift donors."

Let's examine each myth separately.

"Most people are too busy and are not interested in being friendly with me"

Some major gift officers like to put it this way: "I would be more diligent in personal donor solicitation if I thought donors' lives weren't so crowded that there was no time for me." This thought shifts the blame for lack of personal contact from the development officer to the prospective donor. *They* are the reason we don't call them. *Their* priorities prevent us from making contact. This attitude coupled with that logic produces a never-ending downward spiral. Therefore, when the development officer finally gathers up the courage to call the prospect, he or she is always amazed when a cordial response is received and a date for a meeting set.

Notice that this myth has its focus on friendship—not getting acquainted, discussing the nonprofit's mission, or listening to the donor's concerns. While friendship is often a byproduct of meeting with prospects, it should not be the objective. A well-known major donor who was addressing a large gathering of development officers shocked her audience by stating, "Let's start out by getting something straight. We are not friends. We never will be. But what we *can* achieve is a close professional relationship over a common concern—your organization. I am in the business of giving my time and financial resources away. You are in the business of securing both."

The audience laughed nervously. Those officers who worked with her were amused because they knew her as a warm, interesting, and interested individual. But her point was an important one. Each party to the solicitation has specific objectives to achieve, and your institution or organization provides the common ground when it can fulfill the prospect's objectives.

If correctly approached, most people will make the time to learn about you and the mission of the organization or institution you represent.

"Most people do not like to talk about themselves"

This myth is diametrically opposed to the adage that "the sweetest sound you will ever hear is the sound of your own voice." People who believe the adage will probably be very boring people. And people who believe the myth will be very lonely people—at least in their professional lives.

Most people love to share their lives with someone who is genuinely interested in hearing about them. While not everyone is ready to reveal his or her personal life, most people are surprisingly responsive to a good listener. The more open you are to listening and drawing others out, the more enthusiastic people will be about sharing with you their accomplishments, hopes, dreams, fears, failures, and current involvements. In a conversation with a prospect, your role as listener is to relax, enjoy the conversation, and seek congruent concerns. This doesn't mean you are seeking to manipulate the donor, but rather to understand his or her objectives and to relate them to the mission of your institution or organization.

"People will reject personal support and attention"

It is hard to see why anyone would believe this particular myth. After all, most of us enjoy personal support and attention and don't consider that this makes us different from everybody else. But perhaps this myth endures because fund raisers question their own motives: Isn't their *real* objective to secure a gift from a prospect, not to give him or her support and attention? Perhaps this objective needs to be reviewed and revised. Another way to look at it is to consider a major gift as being one of the possible byproducts of establishing a relationship with a donor.

A personal experience of mine received national attention when it was featured as a cover story in CASE CURRENTS a few years ago. An elderly woman used to call me every couple of weeks to inquire if I would be "out in her area in the next day or two." She was a supporter of the college I represented, and I genuinely enjoyed her company. We always set a time to visit. She usually wanted to drive to the supermarket advertising the lowest price on bananas. One day I joked, "Did it ever occur to you that you could afford to buy the market or perhaps a plantation?" She replied, "Maybe so, but then I wouldn't have *you* to share my pursuit of the best buy."

Cheap bananas were not the issue. Trust-building through personal support and attention was the issue for both of us. Some years later her major gift bequest to the college was the result of someone honoring her need.

We are all alike in that we enjoy the support and the supporter. Our task as major gift officers is to conduct ourselves as if personal support and attention are an expectation, not an exception.

"If I could learn 'the right words to say,' then I would be more successful in calling on major gift donors"

If you think that certain words are responsible for securing gifts, you may find yourself focusing on the verbal aspects and ignoring all the other nonspoken—but very important—elements of the gift solicitation process. This myth could make you into an actor rather than an individual.

As you will see in later chapters, some ways of presenting a gift opportunity are better than others. You can reduce the discomfort level for both parties by choosing your phrases with care. But words should not occupy center stage. Building relationships, establishing mutual trust, seeking answers, and solving problems take precedence over any "magic words."

Major gifts are secured because donors come to the conclusion that their objectives are satisfied by saying "yes" to your request. Enlightened self-interest and the needs of the nonprofit come together to produce mutual satisfaction.

Confronting—and dispelling—these four myths should be accompanied by an honest examination of your own attitudes. If you reject each of these myths, both intellectually and through your actions, solicitation can become the most enjoyable part of your responsibilities.

Chapter 5

Understanding the Sources of Interpersonal Communication

Before you address pre-visit communication steps and strategies, you need to understand the communication process itself. This can help you improve your communication abilities and style. According to Professor David K. Berlo, all communication is made up of five basic components:
- communication skills;
- attitude;
- knowledge;
- social system;
- culture.[1]

These sources intermingle to form communication. Let's look at each source individually.

Communication skills

Each of us begins with a different communication skill level, and these differences become apparent very early in life. A child may be known as a "good listener" or blessed with "the gift of gab." These labels become self-reinforcing, both positively and negatively. As the child receives encouragement through positive labels, he or she refines and improves those traits. Conversely, the child sets up defenses to negative labels that also influence communication skill levels.

As communicators, most of us have a mix of positives and negatives. Think of the members of your own family, your friends, and your professional colleagues. What are their strengths and weaknesses as communicators? How does your assessment of a person's communication skills affect your relationship with him or her?

Possibly the most important point for our purposes is that no one communication skill level or ability is a prerequisite for success in major gift fund raising. Many major gift development officers who appear to be quiet or shy are actually very successful, as are others who are talkative, outgoing personalities. Personality type and communication skill level are not the same, even though the distinction between the two sometimes appears to be blurred. But they do overlap. For example, a person who is naturally introverted but has learned to be more extroverted is often extremely successful as a communicator. Consider those of your colleagues who are successful in major gift fund raising. What is their communication skill level? How would you describe their personalities?

As you can see, neither skill level nor personality type is the determining factor in fund-raising success. A low communication skill level is not fatal, nor a high one a guarantee of success.

Attitude

Your attitude has a major influence on how you communicate and how that communication is received and perceived. What is your attitude toward your job? Do you view your responsibilities positively? Does your job bring any joy into your life?

A planned gift officer was having a terrible time establishing himself in his chosen profession. This was a major disappointment to him and a mystery to the nonprofit organization that had hired him. His background and experience were strong indicators of success as a planned giving officer. One day in the midst of a training session for individuals new to planned giving, the class members were asked for their views regarding various types of charitable gift instruments. The officer blurted out, "Planned gifts are designed to rip off the government and low-income taxpayers." He was embarrassed by his comment, and the class was stunned. After extensive discussion, he acknowledged that his negative attitude had had a major influence on his communication with planned gift prospects. Eventually, the planned gift officer took a job in admissions in a private college where he is achieving great success in a field he considers "important to the nation's future."

What is your attitude toward philanthropy and the distribution of wealth? Your attitudes in these areas will have a major influence on how you communicate with your prospective donors. Your comfort level or lack of comfort will be determined by your attitude.

Your profession requires you to work with wealthy individuals and agents of wealth. Does that positively or negatively impact you? Many major gift officers find the selfless nature of philanthropy a major attraction to working with prospective donors. The Will Rogers syndrome ("I never met a [philanthropist] I didn't like") would certainly be a positive influence on your attitude and thus your communication.

Knowledge

As discussed in Chapter 3, fear of lack of knowledge can be a barrier to effective communication. Your knowledge about the broad area of development serves as an important communication source. Knowledge enables you to exchange information and seek additional information with relative ease and comfort. Lack of knowledge about the subject has the opposite effect. You may fear that you will be exposed for your limited understanding of the subjects under discussion.

On the other hand, assumed knowledge has great negative potential. It is very dangerous to infer anything about a potential donor based upon partial information. Let's say, for example, you review your office research file and learn that the prospect served in the armed forces, intelligence branch, before spending five years at a private "think tank" on war strategy. Because you have been to the prospect's manufacturing plant, you know that she prides herself on having the largest American flag in the county flying on the building's rooftop.

Is it safe to assume that she favors a strong national defense strategy? Is she likely to be unhappy that students at the university you represent are staging a peace rally? Do not infer anything prior to your meeting. Ask her to tell you how she feels about these matters. You listen, she talks, you learn. Both parties become more knowledgeable about each other.

Social system

Your social systems—your active body of beliefs—form a large portion of the source of your communication. We have each had a "lifetime of learning," acquiring opinions on a wide range of subjects. Some opinions are valid, some are not, but all are held with great conviction.

Philanthropist Arnold Beckman has often said he would like to take his last breath and give away his last dollar at the same time. This opinion is strongly held and influences his gift pattern and the timing of his gifts. What is important to understand is how Beckman arrived at his conclusions regarding his duty to give back his resources to the scientific community that he has made such an important part of his life.

Try a test to compare your social system with that of a friend or colleague. Be quick. Don't reflect on what is socially acceptable. This is *your* personal social system jumping out. Write your one- or two-word reaction to the following list:

- Californians;
- the Deep South;
- redheads;
- people who wear bow ties;
- farmers.

Do not defend your answers, but compare them with those of your friend. Now reflect on what events in your life have helped form your beliefs. Later on, you'll consider methods of learning this same information about a prospective donor.

Culture

This last communication source is similar to your social system. Here you focus on the influence of environment on communication. Where were you raised? Under what circumstances? What are your recollections of your childhood? How does that time compare with your present circumstances? What is it about your present environment that most strongly affects you? Answering these questions will provide important discoveries about yourself and about those with whom you communicate.

Like social systems, culture is an important source of communication. These elements have strong interplay with one another to determine how you "see" and hear what is being discussed. Understanding the interplay and using that understanding to interpret messages is a valuable communication tool.

These five elements form the source of communication. Each of us is influenced by them in every word we speak.

Note

[1] David K. Berlo, *The Process of Communication* (New York: Holt, Rinehart and Winston, 1960), 72.

Chapter 6

Barriers to Effective Communication in Major Gift Solicitations

Although each major gift solicitation situation is different, similar problems tend to surface. Before you visit a prospect, you can prepare by trying to anticipate potential problems. The following checklist can help you identify the most frequent communication problems:

Differing images

Problems will arise if you and the prospect see the communication situation in different ways. Ask yourself the following questions:

1. What is my purpose in communicating? Will the prospect think I am trying to put something over on him or her?

2. What is my job function? Does the prospect believe that my task is to raise the most money possible for my institution?

3. What is my image of benevolence? What is the prospect's?

4. What is my picture of the prospect? Does this concur with the prospect's self-image?

5. How sympathetic am I to his or her needs? Am I problem-centered or solution-centered?

Bypassing

Two-way communication is essential in face-to-face solicitation. Use the following questions to assess your ability to listen aggressively.

1. Do I ask open-ended questions to encourage the prospect to express his or her worries and opinions?

2. Do I really care about what he or she has to say? Does the prospect see me as a talker but not a listener?

3. Do I practice role reversal? Do I attempt to see things from the donor's point of view? Do I restate unclear ideas to be sure that I understand the prospect's thoughts?

4. Do I listen without interrupting—even when the prospect is criticizing or stating something that I believe to be untrue?

Ambiguity

Do you and the prospect speak the same language? The prospect won't agree to your proposal if he or she doesn't understand it.

1. Does the prospect understand technical development terms, such as "capital gift," "deferred gift," and "endowment"? Have I thought about how to explain these terms to others? Do I use visual aids?

2. Do I ever assume that because *I* know the meaning of a word, the prospect must know it also?

Faulty language

It's important to be aware of what language *can* and *cannot* do. Although words are not everything in a conversation with a donor, they *are* important, and how you use them can make the difference between effective communication and misunderstanding. Assess your language skills with the questions below:

1. Do I organize what I have to say around a few main points?

2. Do I separate facts from inferences?

3. Do I assume that words are "things" or that they perfectly represent or describe "things"? Do I assume that all words mean the same to all people?

4. Do I use analogies and examples to clarify terms?

5. Do I present either too much or too little information at one time?

6. Do I avoid jargon, poor grammar, regional expressions?

Lack of trust

What you say and do during the solicitation will have little effect if basic trust is missing. Do prospects feel at ease with you? If they do, you are probably able to give an affirmative answer to all of the questions below.

1. Do I make a favorable first impression? Am I personable, warm, friendly? Am I poised, interested, enthusiastic? Am I neatly groomed?

2. Do I trust others? Do I trust the prospect?

3. Do I seek to win belief rather than arguments? Are my appeals based on criteria that the prospect can accept? Do I use the implicative approach—working from points on which the prospect agrees to more controversial aspects?

4. Do I avoid talking down to a prospect?

5. Do I use facts and specific examples? Are they accurate and not exaggerated?

Style of delivery

What you wish to communicate may look good on paper but is it persuasive in practice? Consider the questions below to assess your delivery skills:

1. Is my voice intelligible? Is it forceful? Flexible? Free from distracting articulation habits?

2. Do I affirm with body language what I say with words? Is my face expressive? Do my hands reinforce what I say, or do I distract the prospect by fidgeting, slouching, pacing, or rocking back and forth on my feet?

3. Do I look the prospect in the eye when I talk *and* when I listen?

Although we have been talking since our earliest years, we can never be completely free from communication problems. Awareness of the barriers you are likely to encounter is the first step toward removing or reducing them.

Chapter 7

Major Gift Solicitation: 10 Steps to Success

In previous chapters, we have discussed the communication process in general. In this chapter, we begin to give some organization to what we've learned. After decades of study by experts in the mechanics of face-to-face communication and years of experience in major gift solicitation by hundreds of development officers, it is clear that certain sequential steps are the key ingredients to a successful major gift solicitation:

1. Develop a clear statement of purpose.
2. Understand the prospect's frame of reference.
3. Determine the prospect's mental set.
4. Ask open-ended questions.
5. Separate facts from inference.
6. Avoid faulty grammar.
7. Avoid jargon.
8. Monitor nonverbal communication.
9. Stay in the information-seeking mode.
10. Develop a list of exit responsibilities.

This chapter examines each of these important steps.

1. Develop a clear statement of purpose

We are all familiar with the Cheshire Cat's comment from *Alice in Wonderland:* If you don't care where you are going, it doesn't matter which way you go. The same is true in the solicitation of a major gift, that is, you need to set forth a clear statement of objectives—your purposes for the meeting with the prospect—before you ask for the appointment. Before the actual visit, you need to review your purpose again to see if it has changed since the time you set the appointment. Has anything happened in the interim that requires revising the purpose? If there has been any change, you should communicate this to the prospective donor by letter, phone, or in person at the beginning of the visit.

To establish your objectives, ask yourself the following questions:

1. Where are you in the cultivation process? Will this be the first meeting with the prospect or are you acquaintances, friends, or colleagues who know each other but have never discussed this particular subject? Have other staff or volunteers visited with this prospect?

2. Are your objectives consistent with the process, project, and prospect?

3. How long will the visit be? A half-hour? An hour? Are the objectives achievable in the scheduled timeframe? Are you moving too slowly? Too quickly?

4. Have you conducted enough research to validate your purpose? The research should be done before you establish the objectives. Once the objectives are set, you should review the research to check for inconsistencies.

5. Is your oral presentation prepared around a few main points? Many solicitation visits are unsuccessful because the objectives are so numerous or so diffuse that the fund raiser cannot focus them into two or three major issues.

Just as you wouldn't take a trip without a roadmap or a timetable, you can't risk a solicitation visit without clear objectives.

Exercise No. 1. Consider the following scenario: You are the new development officer at the law school, and you are preparing to visit Ms. Black, an attorney. Ms. Black is an alumna of the law school, class of 1960. She regularly returns for the annual Dean's Lecture and is a good friend of the current law school dean, Dr. White. She has never volunteered any time, although she has been asked on several occasions. When she declines, she always cites a "fantastically heavy caseload."

Your research reveals that she is highly regarded as a litigation attorney and defends many of the large corporations in your area. The dean estimates Ms. Black's annual income to be in the $250,000-400,000 range. She lives quite modestly. You have never met her, but Dean White feels it would be prudent for her to "get to know our new development officer."

A campaign to establish a chair in honor of Dean White, who retires in two years, is scheduled to begin in eight months. You are hopeful that Ms. Black will serve on the major gifts committee (gifts of $25,000 to $50,000) and give a leadership gift of $30,000 over three years. Her previous giving history has been limited to a $1,000 annual gift to support student fellowships. Please complete Assignments A and B (the assignments are discussed at the end of this chapter).

Assignment A: Write out the objectives for your visit.

Assignment B: You have called Ms. Black for an appointment. Now prepare a brief opening dialogue.

2. Understand the prospect's frame of reference

Research suggests that we communicate more easily with people who share our experiences, value systems, vocabulary, knowledge, and assumptions than with people who don't. Life experiences affect how a person "frames"—

or interprets—what he or she hears in a conversation. We refer to this as *frame of reference.*

Both parties' comfort levels increase when common background and experiences form the basis of their conversation. For example, it is usually easier for two fiscal conservatives to understand each other when discussing the economy than a conservative and a liberal socialist. For this reason, it is imperative that you understand the prospect's frame of reference very early in the conversation.

As a major gift officer, you are not required to agree with the prospect's views, but you should understand the references that frame those views. When you do, respect for differences is the result. You might not agree, but you can say, "I know where you're coming from."

Exercise No. 2. You are meeting for the first time with Mr. and Mrs. James, retired farmers who now live near the hospital where you serve as the major gift officer. Research on the Jameses is nil. They have both been patients for routine medical purposes and have donated annually to the children's cancer center. Annual gifts have ranged from $1,200 to $4,800.

Assignment: Develop two or more questions that will help you understand the Jameses' frame of reference.

3. Determine the prospect's mental set

We see and hear what we expect to see and hear. How do the development officer and the prospect see each other? And what does each expect the other to say and do? The answer depends on what each person is "set" to see. We call this phenomenon *mental set.*

Television networks are very aware of the self-reinforcing nature of mental set. Voices announce that you are "going to love the network's new 8 o'clock show." The preview of the upcoming offering appears with jokes and a loud laugh track. Valuable air time is spent conditioning us to expect an enjoyable experience.

At the opposite extreme, a mental set to expect a negative experience can be very powerful. You say, "I'm not looking forward to the party Friday night. I'm sure it will be boring and I'll have a terrible time." You are mentally set to reinforce your preconditioned view, and chances are, you *will* have a miserable evening.

It is important, if possible, to discover the prospect's mental set before your meeting. Research in this area will help your communication go well.

Once in face-to-face contact with the prospect, it is important that you verify all the inferences you have gained from pre-meeting research. This can best be accomplished through questions that keep the prospect talking in the early part of the interview. If you have determined that the prospect's mental set is not what you had expected, you have two choices:

• attempt to alter it; or

• orient your comments and ideas—the communication you send—so that they fit with the prospect's mental set.

Determining mental set, as in understanding frame of reference, requires patience and sharp listening skills.

Exercise No. 3. Janet Hamilton is a computer company executive who has climbed the executive ladder rapidly. You have never met her, but you know from the files that she has supported the symphony foundation you represent. At a recent concert she complained to an executive board member of the foundation that "the symphony is out of touch with its supporters." Ms. Hamilton is a longtime season subscriber, but has never given a gift to the symphony. The board member suggests that you "make an appointment and straighten out her views!" You schedule an appointment for you *and* the board member to meet with Ms. Hamilton.

Assignment A: List negative and positive examples of a typical development officer's mental set about donors and the philanthropic process.

Assignment B: List negative and positive examples of a typical donor's mental set about development officers and the philanthropic process.

Assignment C: Prepare four questions that would help you discover Ms. Hamilton's mental set.

4. Ask open-ended questions

Questions can serve as a conversation traffic light. A bipolar question—one that can be answered "yes" or "no"—can stop the flow of communication. An open-ended question can provide the future direction for continuing the interchange. Consider the conversation below between a major gift officer and a prospective donor:

Officer: Have you heard of our project to help the homeless?

Donor: Yes.

Officer: I'm sure you feel the homeless problem is important.

Donor: Yes.

Officer: Would you like me to tell you about our project?

Donor: Yes, please do.

On the surface the interchange seems successful. The prospect has heard of the nonprofit's work, feels the problem is important, and wants to hear more about the project. But is any real communication taking place? What has the prospect heard about the project? Why does the prospect feel the problem is important? Where does this problem rank in the prospect's priorities? Is the gift officer learning anything about the listener's readiness to "hear" about this important project?

To elicit more information, use open-ended questions. Open-ended questions begin with "how," "why," and "tell me...." Let's consider the same conversation with open-ended questions:

Officer: What have you heard about our homeless project?

Donor: [Replies, revealing his or her knowledge of the project and opinions about it, perhaps comparing it to similar projects.]

Officer: You seem very knowledgeable about the problem. How does the homeless project compare with other problems we face?

Donor: [Reply reveals his or her priorities and previous experiences.]

Officer: Tell me what I might tell you about our project that would be helpful to you.

Donor: [Reply focuses on areas of his or her concern.]

The outcomes of these two conversations are significantly different. The major gift officer knows much more about the prospective donor. The donor has revealed his or her feelings about the project as well as the problem of the homeless in general. At the conclusion of the second conversation, the officer is better able to prepare a proposal that meets this prospect's needs, biases, and priorities.

Exercise No. 4. You are on your way to meet with Mr. and Mrs. Dickinson. You are thinking about the conversation you will have with them and what you would like to know about them. Rewrite the questions below so that they are open-ended questions.

1. Did anyone in your family attend our school?
2. Did you know we have a "grateful patients' fund?"
3. Are you retired?
4. Do you have children?
5. Do you think the welfare system is adequately funded?

5. Separate facts from inference

Making an inference about a prospect without verifying it can be dangerous. For example, is your knowledge of the donor often based on second-hand, written opinions of the hearsay of third parties? This situation is complicated if the donor has a longer relationship with the institution or organization than you do.

It's tempting to believe that intelligent people don't make inferences. But we all make inferences—it's part of the human condition. For example, take a moment to consider the following terms and write your quick, first-impression responses:

- higher education;
- welfare;
- the IRS;
- environmentalists;
- social activists.

Now ask a good friend or close colleague to respond to the same list and compare the responses. Do you make inferences? Yes! Are they warranted? Perhaps—but not always.

After reviewing all the research material on the prospect and carefully conducting interviews with mutual acquaintances, you are ready to prepare a profile. Your information is a composite based on a wide variety of data. Now this information needs to be verified carefully, through cross-checking written material, but also directly with the prospect. Of course, you can't do this in an obvious manner, but rather more subtly, through carefully thought-out questions and, most important of all, through careful listening.

6. Avoid faulty grammar

There is less emphasis on grammar in today's teaching than in earlier years. Prospective major donors, however, are likely to be among the older population, who were schooled in the importance of good grammar. Many of these people are likely to perceive spoken grammar as an indication of the quality of a person's education and written grammar as an indication of the amount of care put into the preparation of a proposal. Although knowing when to use "who" or "whom," "I" or "me," and "can" or "may" may seem insignificant compared to the other communication priorities under discussion, the prospect who notices grammatical errors may draw his or her own negative inferences that can subvert the whole purpose of the appointment. Poor grammar can undermine the best idea, the greatest need, and the most carefully constructed case for support.

7. Avoid jargon

With each passing day, we find more jargon in the advancement/philanthropy field. Words we use every day may have little or no meaning to people outside the profession, including major donor prospects.

If you use a word that is not familiar to the prospect and then fail to explain it, you greatly reduce the possibility of effective communication. For example, you announce that a capital campaign is going to start in six months. But the prospect associates a capital campaign with bricks-and-mortar needs and has no interest in making a gift for this purpose. If the prospect fails to ask for clarification of a term and the conversation continues, you have also set up in the prospect's mind the possibility that his or her ignorance of the exact meaning of the term will be revealed later. The prospect may focus on this problem, rather than the proposal on which you have spent so much time and care.

To avoid the negative consequences of jargon, guard against its usage. This can be accomplished by defining each term or using an appropriate analogy. Meaningful communication will not take place if the prospect and the development officer do not speak the same language.

Exercise No. 5. You are about to pay a call on a wealthy couple who came here from South Korea five years ago. They are very enthusiastic about your college, where their eldest son is a junior, but they are self-conscious about their English. They are particularly confused by slang and jargon.

Assignment: List 15 of the most common jargon terms used in a major gift solicitation. Develop alternate words or analogies for each one.

8. Monitor nonverbal communication

As the axiom states, "One cannot *not* communicate." Words are not required for communication to take place. Over 90 percent of our communicated impact on others may take place nonverbally. All of our senses are active partners in communication. We employ voice, body movements, touch, and space to transmit and receive messages. Clothes and jewelry also transmit nonverbal messages. In short, the communication "recipe" is a small amount of verbal and a large measure of nonverbal ingredients. Both are mixed well with the uniqueness of each personality.

Nonverbal communication plays a very significant role in the success—or lack of success—of face-to-face contact with major gift prospects.

J. Donald Ragsdale, professor of speech communication at Louisiana State University, is well-known as a speaker and teacher to fund-raising professionals. As a former fund raiser himself, he brings the insights both of theory and of practice to major gift fund raising. He has suggested the following as 10 steps to communication failure—or disharmony through "listening."

1. Avoid eye contact. Looking another person in the eye shows receptiveness to the person and his or her thoughts, fostering trust and openness. Avoidance of eye contact produces uneasiness; it might even create a measure of fear and some degree of anger in the other.

2. Refute the other's points. A subtle but effective stratagem is to do this through a running *mental* monologue. Silently find fault with word choices, facial expressions, physical demeanor. Decide that the other person's statements of feelings and/or thoughts are petty, and that all opinions different from your own are illogical. Through this step you can dismiss not only the entire speech, but the speaker as a thoughtful, respectable individual. Most people are reasonably perceptive; your scorn will be noted.

3. Think about other things. No one else has a new perspective to share with you; you can use the time when another is speaking to review your plans for the day. Think back to your earlier meeting with the boss and assess its impact on your future. Plan to call the repair shop and the telephone company as soon as this other person runs down. The other person might recognize your preoccupation; he or she might even point it out. Lie about it. He or she will then not only feel demeaned by your inattention, but will also be uncertain of his or her ability to "read" you.

4. Assign your own meanings. If the other tells you that he or she is confused, deduce that "confused" really means "angry." If the other describes a problem with X, be certain that he or she really means Y but is beating around the bush. Believe that little or nothing he or she says is the real issue; you can read between the lines. This will produce communication chaos in a hurry, particularly if the other is also assigning his or her meanings to *your* speech!

5. Create distance. When a conversation begins with you and another nearby, stand up and walk around. Put as much space between you and the speaker as possible. If you fail to do this, you might experience rapport and solidarity, which will make the other feel that he or she matters to you and is a capable and significant person. This will undermine you, wrecking your reputation as an iceberg.

6. Stay busy. Do anything and everything during another's statements. Sort the mail, make notes on your calendar, draw up lists. Although this step is similar to step no. 3, it is a separate rule. It informs the other of his or her great luck in getting time with you, making him or her insignificant in comparison. Should the other comment on your doing things, be surprised. Observe coolly that capable people can do several things at a time without a loss of focus. When he or she knows that you consider him or her a simpleton, disharmony is assured.

7. Maintain a poker face. Even small animals depend upon "reading" situations for comfort and survival; humans have the same need. Deprive others of this natural privilege by revealing as little as possible of your emotions. If the other says something humorous, maintain a steady face. If the other hits close to home in a statement, remain detached and dispassionate. A display of feelings could contribute to the other's recognition of your humanity; he or she might extend warmth and understanding.

8. Be silent. "Silence is the sovereign contempt." (But if anyone should say this to *you,* respond with "Silence is golden.") Ask no questions to clarify the other's points. Restate nothing to determine real meanings. Especially avoid participating through providing appropriate examples of your own. This would display real understanding of the issues.

9. Respond to distractions. Any distraction will do. Notice that the other's hair is parted differently and remark upon it while the other is talking. Hear voices in another room and wonder aloud about what is going on in there. The other party will get the message that you don't care a whit about his or her issues.

10. Close early. Assure the other that you "get the picture" before he or she has had adequate opportunity to make the point. Say that you agree and that you will address the problem starting right now. Thank him or her for bringing it to your attention, smile confidently and confidentially, then get out of the situation any way you can. If possible, leave the room with something in your hand as if you have urgent business elsewhere. This is a proven method of frustrating others and creating doubts about your credibility.

Although most of us would never do any of these intentionally, in your busy and stressful life you may, to your surprise and dismay, find yourself in a situations where you are taking one of these steps to communication failure. Becoming aware of the behavior should lead to its immediate correction.

Exercise No. 6. Ragsdale recommends this exercise to understand the role of nonverbal communication in your conversation. Select a colleague to play the role of a major gift prospect. Ask him or her to do each of the following as you talk.
1. Look at the floor.
2. Stare at your face.
3. Glance around.
4. Stare at your waist.
5. Maintain comfortable eye contact.
Discuss your reactions to each behavior.

9. Stay in the information-seeking mode

One of the hardest parts of interpersonal communication is to listen and learn and *keep on* listening and learning until you have established in your own mind the prospect's frame of reference and mental set. A good rule to follow is, "I will keep listening and asking open-ended questions until I am confident I understand the prospect enough to avoid making unwarranted inferences."

Do not "leap over" listening to make a prepared pitch. If you have not heard and understood what the prospect is saying, you cannot offer a proposal for support that has a reasonable chance of receptive consideration.

10. Develop a list of exit responsibilities

Once you have developed the skills to better communicate the needs of your institution or organization, you will begin to relax and enjoy both the process and the prospect. The more experienced you become, the more enjoyment you will derive from face-to-face contact.

While a relaxed nature is a real communication "plus," it should not detract from your purpose of representing the needs and mission of your nonprofit. During nearly every conversation, you will make promises to perform certain tasks—to send information or to secure additional information. These promises present you with the opportunity to build a higher trust level. Lack of follow-through tells the prospect in the strongest way possible that he or she is not important to you or to your organization or institution.

At the end of every face-to-face contact with the prospect, you should agree verbally (and write it down!) on who will do what to facilitate the gift process. This agreement forms the basis for future meetings and continued contact.

This chapter has focused on 10 steps to conducting the successful solicitation of a major gift. We have, in most cases, just skimmed the surface and introduced the ideas. Many of the steps require practice to understand their relevance and apply the principles. Role-playing simulated conversations with prospects will enhance your ability to communicate. Select trusted friends or professional colleagues and role-play cultivation or solicitation situations. You can begin your sessions with the cases offered in Section 2 of this book.

Discussion of exercises

Exercise No.1. Assignment A: Your objectives might include the following:

1. Become acquainted and establish rapport with Ms. Black.

2. Thank her for previous gifts and report the status of the student fellowship fund.

3. Find out her views on the priority of student fellowships.

4. Determine her feelings about Dean White, her leadership, and the current direction of the law school.

5. Introduce the idea of the forthcoming campaign to establish the Dean White Chair.

Your primary objective is to become acquainted. Ms. Black has already established relationships with both the dean and the law school; you are the new person in this scenario. Your second objective is to acknowledge Ms. Black's past support and to "steward" the gifts by reporting on their use.

Objective no 3 is extremely important. You know that the institution hopes to shift Ms. Black's focus to an academic chair. But before presenting this idea, you must determine whether student fellowships are *her* priority.

Objective no. 4 attempts to avoid accepting the inference that Ms. Black is enthusiastic about Dean White's leadership (see Step No. 5). The answer seems to be "yes," but unless you verify (or disprove) this inference, it could sidetrack your overall objective.

In objective no. 5 you are introducing an idea, not a set plan. You and the dean may wish to tailor your follow-up appeal to Ms. Black's reactions and comments.

Assignment B: Your opening remarks should include the following points:

Officer: Ms. Black, this is Robin Green. I'm the new development officer at State Law School. Thank you for taking my call. I know how very busy you are . . . .

Ms. Black: [She replies.]

Officer: Dean White suggested I stop by and get acquainted. She has told me many good things about you, your practice, and your support for her and the Law School. Would an appointment in the next two or three weeks for a half-hour meeting fit your schedule?

Ms. Black: [She replies. You and she agree on a time, date, and place.]

Officer: Great! I'll look forward to meeting you and updating you on the latest news at the Law School . . . .

Now you have communicated your objectives. They should be repeated when you meet. Remember to verify how long you have to meet, both on the phone and at the beginning of the meeting. (This is usually not as important for visits in the home.)

Exercise No. 2. Your inquiry might include the following questions:

1. I understand you farmed in this area. Please tell me about it.

2. How do you feel about the current state of agriculture?

3. How did the two of you meet?

4. Tell me about your family.

5. The hospital really appreciates your support. We couldn't carry on the quality of care without the generosity of people like you. Thank you very much. I'm interested in why you've chosen the children's cancer center.

Notice that each inquiry invites a wide-ranging response. Each can be followed up with questions within the subject area, as the conversation naturally flows. As you begin to understand the Jameses' frame of reference, you may also wish to explore why they moved from the farm to a location so near the hospital.

Exercise No. 3. *Assignment A:* A typical development officer's mental set toward donors—and philanthropy—might include the following negative responses:

1. They will give if I say the right thing.

2. They will give if I use the right technique.

3. They should share their wealth by giving to our need.

4. They owe us/the community.

5. The cause is just, but I feel like a beggar.

Positive responses might include:

1. They will respond favorably if I can connect our need and their priorities.

2. They are fortunate to have financial resources to share.

3. I am fortunate to be able to represent such a worthy cause.

4. Generally, donors are good, caring people.

Assignment B: A donor might have the following negative mental set toward development officers and philanthropy:

1. They want money for their cause.

2. They think I'm rich.

3. They need money now.

4. If I give, they'll come back for more.

5. They like me only for my money.

Positive responses could include:

1. I hope they can meet my needs.

2. I am fortunate to have financial resources to share.

3. Our community is better off because of this organization's work.

4. Perhaps they also need volunteers.

Assignment C: Here are some examples of the kind of questions that might help you discover Ms. Hamilton's mental set:

1. You've been a longtime symphony subscriber. How would you describe your experience so far?

2. Could you compare your present experiences with the symphony with your experiences in previous years?

3. We are a volunteer-led organization. Your views are important. You shared your view that we are out of touch with our supporters. We're interested in hearing more about your feelings.

4. Obviously, you have given a great deal of thought to the symphony. How would you feel about volunteering some time to help us?

Exercise No. 4. You might rewrite the "yes" or "no" questions in this exercise as follows:

1. Tell me about any past associations you or your family has had with our school.

2. What have you been told about our Grateful Patients' Fund?

3. Tell me about your career.

4. Tell me about your family.

5. How do you feel about the current funding of the welfare system?

Chapter 8

Understanding and Motivating Major Gift Prospects

E ach prospect walks an individual path as he or she processes the decision
whether or not to make a major gift to your institution. Various motivational
factors enter into this decision. Different personal need-fulfillment factors
are also "in play" during the cultivation and solicitation. If you are to improve
your proficiency as a solicitor, you need to understand donors' needs. Once you
develop an understanding of these needs, you can develop motivational responses.

David Dunlop, director of capital projects at Cornell University, is one of
the most respected teachers/practitioners in the profession. In Developing
an Effective Major Gift Program, Dunlop states, "Regular gifts and ultimate
gifts are made for a number of divergent reasons. However, it is almost always
a personal and deep sense of commitment that motivates the giver to make
an ultimate gift. This commitment has been nurtured by experiences that
developed the giver's *awareness, understanding, caring, involvement,* and
sense of commitment."[1]

Motivational factors

Karen Osborne, vice president for development at Trinity College, has elo-
quently taught CASE audiences that the two major factors motivating positive
major gift decisions are the donor's strong identification with the institution and
his or her close involvement with an individual associated with the institution.

The first factor, strong identification with the institution, is typically built
over several years and is the result of carefully planned cultivation. During
this time the donor becomes aware of the mission and priority needs of the
institution. Gradually the focus of the donor narrows from general institutional
needs to specific programmatic or facility needs.

Let us consider Joan Smith, class of 1950, a longtime active alumna of the
college. Joan has given increasingly larger sums to the alumni association's

annual fund. She served two terms on the alumni association board of directors before being invited to serve a six-year term on the college's board of trustees. Currently, she chairs the financial aid committee.

Joan has enjoyed significant success in the development of nutritional supplements and weight loss programs. She wrote a best-selling book entitled *To Your Health: Facts and Fads*. She is a close friend of the college's president, Carol Thomas-Sisson. Their common interest in providing financial support to women returning to complete their degrees has provided noteworthy progress in this area.

Recently the trustees adopted the academic council's recommendation to concentrate on private support to scholarships and fellowships. The goal of the comprehensive campaign, entitled "Students First," is to raise $10 million over three years.

As Joan is returning from an estate planning meeting with her attorney and CPA, she begins to reflect on the important role the college has played in her life and in the lives of friends and professional colleagues. Later, Joan tells a former classmate, "It's payback time. It's my turn at the plate."

Joan's story is typical of many major gift prospects who, over a long period of time and involvement, discover an ever-deepening bond with the institution. The job of the major gift officer is to help Joan realize her philanthropic objectives.

The second factor, close involvement with an individual associated with the institution, encompasses highly personal factors and relationships rather than identification with the institution itself.

John Fisher majored in civil engineering at the university. He graduated in 1940 and joined the Army during World War II. While John was overseas, the dean of the school of engineering, Mel Ashcroft, kept up a steady correspondence with him. Dean Ashcroft's letters always seemed to arrive during periods of loneliness for John, when he longed to "hear from his roots."

When the war ended, John started his own firm which, over the years, he built into a highly successful civil engineering business. Six of his 14 associates are also graduates of the university's School of Engineering. He considers them "a cut above" his other employees.

The engineering school's development officer, Janet Caruso, was having lunch with John at his firm's cafeteria when she first heard the story of the wartime correspondence with the late Dean Ashcroft. Janet remarked, "You know, our current dean, Bob Muncie, is a caring individual too. He always seems to have former students in his office. I don't know how he finds the time."

Janet Caruso arranged a meeting with John and Dean Muncie. They hit it off immediately. Philanthropy was not part of the discussion. John had given $500 a year to the Class of '40 Fund and had rejected all requests for additional gifts. As the meeting concluded, Dean Muncie remarked, "John, I'm glad you told me your story about Mel Ashcroft. If the Board of Regents approves our plan to name the new building Ashcroft Hall, I'd like to tell your story at the ground-breaking."

At this point, John remembered an earlier phone call from Janet who had wanted to meet to discuss a "building naming opportunity." He began to wonder if he had acted hastily in rejecting the meeting.

Strong relationships within the context of an institutional setting are commonplace. Our job as major gift officers is to seek out and identify these relationships and to explore their potential as a motivation for philanthropy.

Responding to prospects' needs

In addition to these two factors, fund raisers should be aware of powerful human needs that are often important considerations in the decision to give a major gift:
1. The need to memorialize or honor oneself or loved ones.
2. The need to perpetuate values or opinions.
3. The need to belong.
4. The need for recognition or status.
5. The need to fulfill perception of duty.

The need to memorialize or honor oneself or loved ones. It is part of the human condition that we must all consider the unavoidable fact of our own mortality. What difference did our life make to our family, friends, and community? Will there be any evidence that we were once a contributing member of this society? What is our legacy? As we strive to come to grips with the fact that life does indeed have a finite measure, we may find comfort in creating a memorial of some sort, either in our own name or in the name of a loved one. A gift to an institution that played a vital role in a donor's life can ensure that future generations take notice of his or her existence.

Our institutions can meet this need by offering the opportunity to name a gift to honor the donor or the donor's designee. The naming opportunity is an outgrowth of the act of philanthropy, not the object of the giving of the gift. The major gift officer needs to understand the donor's wish in this area as it may have much to do with the gift decision.

The need to perpetuate values or opinions. A donor's desire to perpetuate his or her values or opinions is closely related to the need to memorialize himself or herself. Both are "after-life issues"—they have to do with what the donor leaves behind. However, the focus here is not on self, but rather on treasured ideas, values, and opinions. A prospect may be asking, "Do others believe as I do?" "Do others know and understand the same values and opinions?" "Are my ideas important to others?" If the prospect's values and opinions fit the academic priorities and mission of your institution, then your institution can answer "yes" to each of these questions. In this case, a naming opportunity may be appropriate.

For example, let's suppose James and Elizabeth Rogers met on your campus in the late 1930s. The Depression affected their lives in many ways. Both had to work their way through school, and they are proud of the fact that they graduated without any assistance from the government. After college, Jim and Betty worked 12-hour shifts when they were starting their first grocery store. Hard work and Betty's uncanny sense of what consumers wanted brought prosperity. This partnership was successful in a variety of related businesses.

Everyone who knows the Rogers well understands their fervently held, politically conservative views. Central to their thinking is that success without government assistance or interference is the key to a robust economy.

Graduate students in the School of Business at your institution are excited about the opportunities offered through the Entrepreneurship Academy. Here is a risk-free chance to design new businesses and create an organizational plan for evaluation by experienced entrepreneurs. The Academy is where Dean Robert Ritchie met the Rogers. Three years ago, Dean Ritchie invited the Rogers to serve as evaluators/partners in the Academy. They agreed eagerly. Betty remarked, "Someone still values hard work, independence, and risk-taking." The Rogers have not regretted their involvement with the Academy.

As the Rogers approached retirement, they began to divest themselves of their numerous business interests. And they started to develop a plan to "help foster important ideas." When Dean Ritchie proposed a major endowment fund to assure the continued vitality and expansion of the Academy through the establishment of the Rogers Family Free Enterprise Endowment, they were very interested in exploring the idea. As John mused, "Maybe our thinking isn't old-fashioned after all."

Throughout the United States many institutions of higher education have established research centers, institutes, and related organizations based on an individual's values or opinions. Major gift officers should always be aware of the possibility of motivating a gift based on the institutionalization of a donor's ideas.

The need to belong. Most of us have from time to time felt that sense of being "alone in a crowd." The room may be full of people, but somehow you don't feel that you're a part of it. We all need some roots or anchors in our lives—some place where we know we belong. The stability of an institution can be very attractive to people seeking such an anchor in today's fast-changing world.

A major gift program with a strong emphasis on donor stewardship will offer many opportunities to become part of the ongoing life of the institution. As donors experience these different aspects of university or school life, they find "welcoming homes." The institution becomes smaller and more personal. As donors sample the menu of choices offered, they find programs that match their interests. This self-selection process forms an important basis for donors to understand the private support needs and opportunities of your institution. The major gift officer's role is to monitor this process and to be ready to make specific gift suggestions at the appropriate time.

The need for recognition or status. Most people enjoy receiving recognition for work well done or deeds accomplished, but the kind of recognition desired varies widely. Many major gift donors prefer—or sometimes even demand—anonymity. But does this mean the gift and the giver go unrecognized? Certainly not! What is important is that you know each donor's needs in this area and attempt to comply with his or her preferences.

For example, a major donor may reject any naming opportunity and all forms of public recognition, but may welcome a small, private dinner with the institution's president and a few friends. Other similar low-key options might be appropriate.

Named gifts are an enormous benefit to the institution. They provide a powerful incentive to others, especially the donor's peers, to consider a similar gift. Named gifts often confer status on the institution, but they do not necessarily indicate a donor's desire for recognition or status. In fact, most donors have to be persuaded to allow their names to be attached to their gift.

Peer recognition is an important motivator for volunteerism and for major gifts as well. It is the major gift officer's job to understand how the donor assesses his or her peers and how accurate this assessment is. When putting together a major gift calling team, the officer needs to have a thorough understanding of the peer structure.

The need to fulfill perception of duty. This motivation is different from those discussed above because it is based on heritage or family expectations rather than the donor's own internal motivations.

Consider the situation in the United States in the late 1800s to early 1900s. Who controlled the bulk of the wealth then? Before the creation of the graduated federal income tax, wealth was concentrated within a few families. Names like Rockefeller, Carnegie, Ford, Huntington, Stanford, and Mellon come to mind. Today, wealth is more widely dispersed throughout the country.

Some of the wealthy people in every community were brought up with the tradition of "giving back to the community." Some were taught from childhood that "our family has a proud history of philanthropy." Such people are motivated to give both by their own expectations and by those of their family. Duty is the primary motivator behind this philanthropy, and the issue is not whether to give but how much and to whom. Who are the "Rockefellers" in your community? What captures their interest? Why? How can your institution move into their scope of concern? You cannot proceed with these prospective donors until you have addressed these questions.

Responding to each of these needs requires that we understand them and that we can differentiate between them. Only then can we understand what may motivate our prospective major donors to act.

Note

[1] David R. Dunlop, "Strategic Management of a Major Gift Program," in Roy Muir and Jerry May, ed., *Developing an Effective Major Gift Program: From Managing Staff to Soliciting Gifts* (Washington, DC: Council for Advancement and Support of Education, 1993), 8-9.

Chapter 9

Getting the Appointment

There are very few points on which fund raisers unanimously agree, but I believe that when asked, most would concur on the answer to the question, "What is the hardest part of your job?" And their answer would be, "Getting the appointment." But getting the appointment—calling a prospect and establishing a time and date to meet face-to-face—is not really the hard part. Nor is the conversation itself. What *is* hard is preparing ourselves psychologically to take the risks involved in this activity. Most people have a tendency to prioritize their activities—to do first those things that have the potential for giving pleasure, and to put off the things that they perceive as being forced upon them. For most people, calling a prospect for an appointment is in the latter category.

This behavior is easy to understand. Calling for an appointment always entails the risk of rejection. The prospect may say, "No, I don't want to meet." Even though this kind of response is very rare, most fund raisers cannot help feeling that their self-esteem is at risk. If the prospect says "no," they feel that *they* are being personally rejected or that their organization is being judged unworthy. It is no wonder most of us put off this call as long as we can.

On the other hand, ask a hundred major gift development officers, "What aspect of your job gives you the most pleasure?" The majority will respond, "Meeting with donors and prospects." What irony! The most distasteful part of the job is calling to set up the most enjoyable part of the job. The reason behind this paradox is that fund raisers really believe the myths regarding major gift solicitation that we discussed in Chapter 4.

The best way to overcome the fear of rejection when calling for appointments is to force yourself to do it on a regular basis. In the beginning, you will be surprised on two counts—first that prospects say "yes," and second that they say "yes" as if they are really looking forward it. After a while, you will become conditioned to expect a positive outcome. By that time, you will have overcome the fear of getting the appointment.

In most cases, in order to make the appointment, you will resort to that most powerful, most widely used, and least understood communication medium—the telephone. Americans have had a long love affair with the telephone, and the thrill of communicating by phone has not diminished over the years. There are over 150 million phones in homes and offices in the United States today. The advent of the mobile cellular phone means that we are almost never out of reach. And most people will interrupt almost any activity to learn the answer to the question, "Who's calling?"

As a fund raiser, your job is to make sure the prospects who answer the phone when *you* are calling are not disappointed. The eight steps outlined below can help you make sure that your call receives the response you want.

Step 1: Conduct prospect research

The first rules of mass marketing are, "Know to whom you are talking. Know his or her name and how to pronounce it. Know his or her relationship (if there is one) to your organization." Following these rules can personalize what might otherwise be a very impersonal activity. When you are calling to set up an appointment with a major gift prospect, these rules apply tenfold, and the personal approach must be genuine.

Begin by reviewing all existing research material, including background profile, updates, and recent debriefing memos. If the material is limited, you will need to interview other staff, volunteers, and mutual acquaintances. Interviewing mutual acquaintances requires tact and diplomacy. You need to make it clear that you are asking questions in order to know the prospect better so that you can determine his or her level of interest in the mission of your institution or organization. You are not looking for confidential information, but rather for basic biographical data that will enable you to personalize the telephone call.

Second, review attendance records to determine if the prospect has attended any events put on by the institution or organization. Often the person you are planning to call is an acquaintance of a donor and has already attended an institutional event as this donor's guest. This is important information and can serve as a basis for further research.

At this point, a sticky situation often arises. Suppose you discover a relationship between your prospect and a volunteer or donor. This person offers to discuss with the prospect his or her enthusiasm for the work of your institution or organization. Encourage this by all means. But if the donor volunteers to call the prospect and introduce you prior to *your* call, you will need to make a quick judgment about the relationship between the donor and the prospect. Will the donor's influence be a positive or negative factor in getting you the appointment? Your decision at this moment can make or break your success with the prospect.

Step 2: Prepare a statement of objectives

For some reason, fund raisers often reverse the steps and prepare the objectives after making the appointment. The reasoning may be, "I'll get the appointment and then I'll decide what to do." Sometimes this is because they don't believe that the appointment will actually be made. But the briefest reflection should reveal that you shouldn't make an appointment with the prospect unless you have a clear purpose in mind.

First, establish the overall objectives of the appointment. These may be one or more of the following:

- initial visit to get acquainted;
- exploration of gift alternatives;
- asking for a gift;
- stewardship/thank you.

The overall objective will determine other objectives. For example, if your overall objective is stewardship, subgoals might include:

- determining the donor's level of satisfaction about the decision to make the gift;
- determining if the stewardship plan was carried out to the donor's satisfaction (public relations, media coverage, thanks, recognition); and
- informing the donor of progress achieved in using gift proceeds.

Step 3: Decide when you can schedule the date

Scheduling the date can be the most difficult part of getting the appointment. You should study your own calendar carefully before you pick up the phone. Determine how flexible you can be in case you need to cancel something on your calendar in order to find a date convenient for the prospect.

If the prospect lives or works fairly close to the institution or organization, you have some leeway in scheduling. The greater the distance, the more limited your appointment options. In addition, the prospect may feel uneasy at the thought that you are willing to travel a great distance to meet with him or her. The prospect may feel that agreeing to a meeting that requires time and expense on your part creates some kind of obligation on his or her part.

Try to allay this fear at the outset. For example, you might say, "I am going to be in Los Angeles in three weeks and would like to meet with you." This relieves the prospect of the time-and-expense pressure and establishes a period of time to set up a meeting. Of course, honesty is the best policy, and if the appointment is the only visit you intend to schedule in Los Angeles, you need to be clear about that too. This at least establishes that the visit is a priority with you.

Always immediately state your overall objective when you are attempting to schedule the date. For example, after introducing yourself, you might say, "I am going to be in your area on June 14 and 15 to meet with alumni of Eastville State, and I would like to stop by to get acquainted." This assures the donor that the purpose of the visit is to get acquainted and *not* (at least at this time) to ask for a gift.

How far in advance you call to make an appointment depends on several factors, including your schedule and that of the prospect; priority of the visit to *both* parties; purpose of the visit; and level of the gift under consideration. The majority of appointments are scheduled at least two weeks in advance and, very often, three or four weeks. A CEO of a major corporation may schedule outside appointments up to six weeks in advance. The major gift officer should attempt to find out the prospect's appointment-setting patterns before calling to set the date of the appointment.

Step 4: Decide how long the visit will be

Establishing how long the visit will be is more important than it might appear. The prospect often bases the decision to agree to a meeting on three factors: the purpose of the visit, the proposed date, and the proposed length of visit. Remember that some professionals, such as attorneys, bill their time on 10-minute intervals. At the other extreme, a retired widower may feel he has all the time in the world. You must honor the time constraints of all prospects, regardless of your perceptions of their availability.

When you begin the conversation to schedule the appointment, try to link all three of these factors. For example, after introducing yourself, you might say, "I'll be in Boston the last week of May to meet friends of the Centerville Museum of Art and would like to meet with you for 45 minutes to discuss your participation in the underwriting of the Monet to Modernism exhibit scheduled for January next year."

Step 5: Plan location

Once the prospect has agreed to the appointment, you will need to establish where the meeting will be held. Location should not be an afterthought, but part of the pre-call planning, and it should depend on the purpose of the visit, your relationship with the prospect, and the nature of the business to be discussed. Visits to get acquainted often take place in the prospect's home or office. This is a setting more comfortable to the prospect and therefore more likely to lead to relaxed conversation. You can learn a lot about a person from his or her surroundings.

If the purpose of the visit is to submit a formal proposal for a major gift, the circumstances may dictate where you meet. For example, if you represent a college or university and the purpose of the gift is to endow the maintenance of the library building, then an on-site meeting will help focus the prospect on the effects of deferred maintenance. If you are requesting a gift for an emergency room addition to the hospital, then an on-site meeting to see afresh the heavy use can serve to reinforce the need.

Other gift requests may be more "site neutral." If you are soliciting travel funds to sponsor an upcoming symphony tour, it probably won't matter whether you meet in the symphony hall or in the prospect's home.

Always let the prospect make the final decision on location. If you have a preference, it should be made as a suggestion. You might say, for example, "Perhaps you would like to visit the recreation center and see the program in action." As you get to know the prospect, you will begin to understand his or her preferences, and the choice of location will become a simple matter.

A volunteer involved in a proposed visit may offer his or her home or office for the meeting. Under certain circumstances this "neutral" site may be a good choice, but you need to understand the relationship of the volunteer and the prospect before you decide to suggest this option.

Step 6: Settle the dining question—to eat or not to eat

Coffee, tea, and cookies are excellent for putting everyone at ease and facilitating the beginning of a first visit. The server establishes himself or herself as host and welcomes the visitor. A full meal, on the other hand, can interfere with a meeting in which the agenda requires a lot of listening and give-and-take. Again, circumstances dictate the choice. The prospect may find it comfortable to invite you to his or her club. This is especially true if the club is part of the prospect's daily routine. Get-acquainted sessions can be enhanced by a meal, but a serious discussion of major gift alternatives is normally not facilitated by a meal unless a particular prospect feels more comfortable making decisions on such matters while eating.

If you agree to meet at a private club, find out if papers can be put on the table. Some clubs have a rule against this, and it would be embarrassing to be asked to remove your materials in the middle of a presentation.

Step 7: Secure the appointment

If you followed Steps 1 through 6, then Step 7 is simple: You just make the call. If you are unable to find a satisfactory time to meet, be sure to ask when you may call back. Seek agreement that you will call again on a specific date. Follow up the call with a written confirmation.

Step 8: Confirm the appointment

Immediately after securing an appointment, you should send a written confirmation that includes:
- thanks for agreeing to meet;
- agreed-on date, time, and place of the meeting;
- purpose of the meeting;
- attendees, if others will be joining you;
- confirmation of any materials either party will prepare for the meeting; and
- commitment to confirm by telephone immediately prior to the meeting.

If you are visiting a prospect whose meetings are arranged by an assistant, be sure that you know the assistant's role in confirming and finalizing the meeting arrangements. Often the key to the meeting with the prospect is becoming acquainted with his or her administrative staff.

Special cases

This chapter has focused on securing an appointment with an individual major gift prospect, but you will also deal with foundations, corporations, and agents of wealth. The circumstances are different in these special cases.

Foundations. Researching a foundation is relatively easy. There is a lot of material available that reveals the formal guidelines under which the foundation operates. Your research should consider:

- the foundation's purpose and its current gift focus;
- gift history—size and purpose;
- emerging areas of interest;
- guidelines regarding visits and proposals;
- program staff assigned to your proposed area of interest; and
- the role of the staff and board in gift decisions.

Foundations are in the business of philanthropy. The question is not whether they will make a gift but to whom the gift will be made. Since foundations are a business, major gift officers often fail to discover the personal side of their operation. But foundations are like individuals—they have a formal and informal side. Get to know the whole operation including:

- the personal likes and dislikes of staff and board;
- the relationships of staff and board to your institution or organization;
- any connections that may exist between your volunteers and the foundation; and
- where or with whom the informal power lies.

If your research does not reveal sufficient information, call the foundation and make inquiries. Be prepared with specific questions that are *not* clearly answered in published information. A phone call to a program officer is the first step in establishing a relationship with a foundation, so it is important to prepare accordingly.

Corporations. Unlike foundations, corporations are in the business of making a profit. Corporate responsibility to the community is not the primary focus. It may be more difficult to determine gift decision-making structure. However, most corporations have a formal gift policy and a process for application.

Remember that a corporation is often guided by enlightened self-interest. A gift that enhances the corporate image, satisfies employees and stockholders, and perhaps has profit implications for the corporation is likely to receive priority consideration.

Decisions regarding major gifts are usually made both top-down and bottom-up at a corporation. If both management and line staff agree that your proposal has merit, you have a good chance of receiving the gift.

With one significant exception, you should follow the same procedure to secure an appointment with a corporate prospect as with an individual. With a corporation, the most important question to answer is with whom should you meet. Many major gift proposals are unsuccessful because they are presented to the wrong people. Your research needs to focus on who makes the philanthropic decisions and how these decisions are processed upward in the corporation.

Agents of wealth. Attorneys, financial planners, and CPAs are called "agents of wealth." These people are often the key to a prospect's major gift decision. The most important rule to remember is that the agent of wealth is employed by the prospect, and therefore any contact with the agent must be facilitated by the prospect and should never take place without his or her permission and knowledge.

Always remember that getting the appointment is the beginning of a beautiful relationship. If you have done the thorough, step-by-step preparation outlined in this chapter, you will be more comfortable when you are making that first telephone call to the prospect.

Chapter 10

The Major Gift Meeting: Opening and Closing Techniques

You've followed the steps recommended in Chapter 9 to secure an appointment with a major gift prospect. Chapter 11 focuses on the meeting itself, but this chapter will help you prepare for it. Note that some of the suggested steps will be more important than others depending on where you are in the cultivation process.

Before the meeting

1. Carefully review your written objectives for the meeting. Has any late information changed these objectives?
2. Review research once again to make sure you are familiar with the details regarding the prospect.

Upon arrival

1. Introduce yourself and immediately present your business card. The prospect can now be confident that he or she will not forget your name, title, or affiliation during the meeting.
2. State your purpose for calling (your overall objective).
3. Listen to the prospect's response. The prospect may change the objectives or misunderstand them. For example, you may need to revise your objectives if:
   - the prospect hands you a sealed envelope containing a gift;
   - another person attends the meeting at the request of the prospect;

• the prospect hands you a copy of his or her written objectives and they differ from yours; or

•the prospect introduces a time schedule that differs from yours.

4. Match your response to the research on the prospect. Obvious errors in research may cause you to revise your objective, but you will need to assure yourself that the new information is accurate.

During the meeting

The following checklist summarizes key communication techniques discussed in other sections of this book:

1. Watch your timing. The prospect will not understand your explanation of your "case" until he or she has seen the importance of listening. You can first demonstrate the importance of listening as you seek information about the prospect's background and experience.

2. Give a short statement of purpose. The prospect will understand better if he or she first gets a "bird's-eye view" of the whole picture.

3. Preview and restate the main points. The prospect can follow an explanation more easily if he or she sees the main parts or divisions.

4. Restate and summarize. Repetition is advisable—but not to the point of boredom. Restate with new details, clarification of obscure aspects, logical deductions, etc. Summarize as you go.

5. Show comparisons. The prospect will understand a new idea best when he or she sees how it is related to an old idea. (This is really the essence of the explanation.)

6. Speak plainly. The prospect can only understand what is stated in his or her language.

7. Be specific and concrete. The prospect will understand best when you deal with specifics. Avoid monotonous abstraction.

8. Narrow the scope. Few people can absorb a lot of information by ear in a short time. Supply "filler" material (at least two examples per point). Keep main points logically related.

9. Vary the approach. The prospect will understand ideas better when he or she sees them from several angles through additional details and materials. Mnemonic devices (formulas, slogans, etc.) can help to emphasize an idea.

10. Give human-interest examples. This is a good way of getting and keeping the prospect's interest.

Close of meeting

Development officers new to major gift fund raising often ask, "When is it time to stop talking and bring the meeting to a close?" The veteran is likely to respond, "You will *know*. You'll just *feel* it." But you will only know or feel that it's time to close if you are alert to what is going on in the conversation.

Monitor the conversation throughout the meeting to be sure the objectives have been covered. When they have been covered, you should probe to determine whether the prospect agrees that the meeting is coming to a close. You might say, "I've enjoyed our meeting and learned a lot about your interesting life. Thanks very much for your time." The prospect will respond to this probe and move to end the meeting or to continue the conversation. When there is agreement that closing is appropriate, you should do the following:

1. Restate the objective of the meeting and review progress. Both parties need to agree on the progress achieved. You could say, "I think we have come a long way in understanding the project. I certainly think I understand your thinking much better. How do you feel?" This is the time to listen to the prospect's response for affirmation of progress.

2. Review new objectives that have arisen during the meeting. Seek understanding on these objectives. Agreement is important.

3. Review expectations of each party. This is the time to check your perceptions. Failure to understand each other at this point would result in very negative outcomes.

4. Set new objectives for the next meeting.

5. Assign responsibilities. During the meeting, you may have made a promise to carry out a task such as research a point, recheck information, or contact certain individuals. The prospect may have agreed to supply a copy of his or her will or prepare a statement of net worth. This is the appropriate time to write down agreed-upon assignments. Agreement on responsibilities forms the basis for the next meeting.

After the meeting

1. Immediately send a thank-you note to the prospect for taking time to meet. Don't wait until you have gathered the information you promised to send. You can always note that you will send the information as soon as you have it.

2. Send written material or call to set a meeting date to review the new information.

3. If other parties are entering the relationship, introduce them in writing *before* they meet with the prospect or contact him or her by phone or letter. Management of the prospect contact team is a key element to a successful outcome.

Remember that a successful meeting is the beginning of the next cultivation step. G.T. "Buck" Smith, a former college president, refers to these steps as "moves." You are moving toward a set goal. You are in a process in which each step is related to another, and the overall success depends on your awareness of where you are in the major gift process and how your current status relates to the overall goal.

Chapter 11

Major Gift Solicitation: The Funnel Technique

C hapter 10 discussed techniques for opening and closing a major gift solicitation meeting. This chapter focuses on the meeting itself. While there is no outline or diagram that can totally structure a conversation between the major gift officer and a prospective donor, the *communication funnel* provides a helpful guideline.

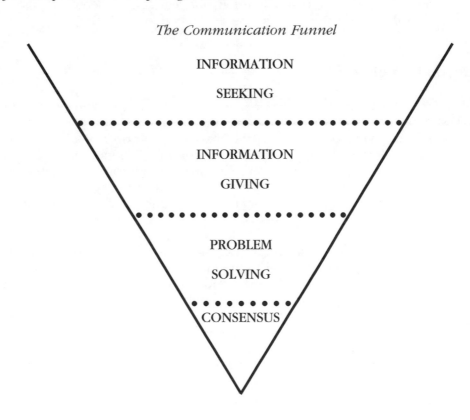

The Communication Funnel

INFORMATION

SEEKING

INFORMATION

GIVING

PROBLEM

SOLVING

CONSENSUS

The funnel provides a visual presentation of the sequential steps in a major gift solicitation. Learning the order of these steps as well as how much time should be devoted to each is critical to effective communication. Let's consider each step:

Information-seeking

Consider this statement: "Every initial interview with a prospective donor should begin with information-seeking. This activity, which is primarily aggressive listening, should constitute 40 percent of the meeting." Sounds logical, doesn't it? Common sense dictates that we cannot work effectively with people until we thoroughly understand them and their needs. Yet in the vast majority of meetings, the talk-oriented "pitch" leaves little opportunity for interruption.

For the past 12 years, I have conducted many seminars nationwide on effective communication. These seminars include a segment of televised, simulated donor interviews. When the red light of the television camera goes on, the lessons on the importance of information-gathering are put to the test. Most major gift officers are able to change their bad listening habits. The 30 percent who cannot are so bound to a habit of talking instead of listening that the "pitch" is as automatic as breathing. In several cases, during televised role-playing, development officers became so agitated by their inability to launch into a pre-planned sales talk that they lost their ability to carry on a normal conversation.

The corporate business world is once again discovering the importance of listening. The nonprofit community cannot afford to forget it. The elementary lessons of the "three L's"—look, listen, and learn—may seem simplistic, but they are the foundation of a successful interview.

Information-giving

Only after you are assured that the prospective donor has told you everything he or she wants to and you have obtained all the information you need for an analysis, are you ready to move to the next step—information-giving. This step supplies information requested by the prospective donor and presents the proposed gift within the frame of reference of the information gathered about the donor's needs. The focus of the conversation is always on the donor rather than on the institution or the organization. Your first concern is to deal with the specifics raised by the donor rather than your desire to present a proposal.

Meshing your answers with the donor's needs is known as *congruency*. Understanding this point is crucial to the interview. Consider the following conversation between a major gift officer and a prospective donor with estate planning problems:

> **Officer:** A while ago you mentioned that you inherited a 500-acre wheat ranch in 1970. Did I understand correctly that the ranch was valued at $200 per acre in your father's estate?

Donor: Well, my sister Gladys inherited 250 acres and I received 500. Yes, the value at that time was $200 an acre.

Officer: That's interesting! Does Gladys still own her portion?

Donor: No, Gladys passed away two years ago and left her part to me.

Officer: I'm sorry to hear that. You must have been close to your sister.

Donor: [Tells long story about this relationship, including other details of the sister's estate.]

Officer: I'll bet the value of the ranch has increased in value since 1970.

Donor: Oh my, yes! My sister's probate listed the value at $1,800 per acre. That's hard to imagine. You certainly can't make a profit farming at those prices.

Officer: Isn't that the truth! You can't make a real profit, and yet, capital gains tax would make it hard to sell.

You probably noticed the following points about this conversation:

1. Even though the conversation is in the information-giving stage, it begins with a question to check the accuracy of earlier information. The question is phrased so that any misunderstanding is the officer's, not the donor's.

2. Once new information is introduced, the officer returns to the information-seeking stage to obtain more data.

3. The problem of capital gains was introduced into the conversation by the officer. The discussion thus becomes personal and solution-oriented.

Again, the important thing to remember is that giving information should be centered on previous information received. This can be done only when you have spent enough time becoming acquainted with and understanding the donor's needs.

Problem-solving

To know whether you are ready for the problem-solving phase of the funnel technique, ask yourself the following questions:

1. Do I have a thorough understanding of the donor?

2. Do I have a complete understanding of the donor's questions and problems?

3. Have I answered all questions to the satisfaction of the donor?

4. Have I proposed satisfactory solutions to those problems that I can help solve?

The process outlined above should bring about an agreement on additional information required and unresolved problems that need to be addressed. Agreement on these items focuses on a solution-oriented conversation. Your challenge is to consider each question until it is answered before proceeding to the next, and last, step—consensus or agreement.

Consensus

Another conversation between the major gift officer and the donor will help you understand this last step in the communication funnel. The focus is still estate planning. The example, which is for illustration only, is not strictly true to life—it excludes the presence of necessary professional parties—but it helps illuminate the process of reaching a consensus with the donor.

Officer: I've analyzed all of the information you so graciously supplied to me two weeks ago. Here is an estate plan that I have prepared. Let's go through it step by step. [Officer explains the plan.] The charitable trust is a key element—in fact, the cornerstone of the plan. How do you feel about the plan and proposed trust?

Donor: It seems to answer all of the problem areas we discussed. However, I think that a trust involving a set number of years, rather than a lifetime, would help me to ensure that my brother Harold is provided for. Even though he is 82 and has an adequate income now, you never know if he may need financial assistance during a major illness.

Officer: Then, if we have your will redrawn and prepare a 20-year charitable remainder unitrust with an 8 percent annual payout, you'll execute the trust?

Donor: Yes, I believe that's what I'll do.

This officer began the funneling process with a broad range of information and systematically narrowed the focus toward possible solutions. This approach saves time and assures each party that all factors were considered in reaching the final decision.

Note that in the above conversation the major gift officer's final question sought to bring closure and agreement. This is a critical point. Two veteran major gift officers were discussing a mutual friend who was unsuccessful as a salesperson. One remarked, "He's bright, articulate, and knows his product." The other replied, "Yes, and he works hard. But he walks by an opportunity to close so fast he never sees it." While there is considerable difference between the profit objectives of salespeople and the problem-solving objectives of major gift officers, this comment is an excellent illustration of our final point: *When all relevant information has been analyzed, when all known problems have been solved, and when an agreement has been reached, pick up a pen and say, "Would you please sign here?"*

Even the most knowledgeable major gift officers become anxious as the time approaches when they must ask the prospect to conclude the discussion and approve the proposed plan. The anxiety increases when it is finally time to ask the donor to sign the necessary papers. If you feel this way, take comfort from the fact that you are not alone. And there is a remedy: You need not be anxious if you are secure in the knowledge that you have followed a process that assures both the donor and your organization or institution that all of their needs have been considered—and that process is the communication funnel.

Years of testing the communication funnel with hundreds of development officers have proven its effectiveness in increasing individual productivity. Understanding the communication funnel and using it wisely can have a tremendous impact on your effectiveness as a major gift officer. Through this technique you can overcome the greatest barrier to effective communication—fear of failure.

Chapter 12

Overcoming Objections: Behind Closed Doors

In our study of a strategic approach to major gift solicitation, we have concentrated on the role of communication in the interaction with the donor; we have walked through the steps of successful solicitation; and, finally, we have covered the solicitation meeting, from getting the appointment to closing the meeting successfully by obtaining agreement on a major gift. But we haven't talked about what happens if the prospect has objections, rejects some aspect of the proposal, or rejects the proposal itself.

For the past eight years, I have chaired a CASE conference entitled "Successful Techniques in Gift Solicitation." When we discuss how to overcome donor objections, it quickly becomes clear that participants' intense interest in objections comes from their fear of outright rejection of the proposal. They often confess, "I am scared to death that the donors will angrily declare, 'No, not now, not *ever* will I consider a gift to your institution!'" The fact that this fear is irrational and without foundation doesn't lessen its intensity. In 20 years of soliciting major gifts, I have *never* encountered an angry, outright rejection, nor do I know any other veteran major gift officers who have.

Then where does this fear come from? Two reasons usually come out when this fear is discussed: First, many people see presentation of a major gift proposal as risking outright rejection of themselves (review the myths covered in Chapter 4) and their profession. Rita Bornstein, president of Rollins College, bluntly states, "People are scared of fund-raising. They see it as begging or they think it's dirty...."[1] The fear of personal rejection becomes magnified despite assurances to the contrary.

The second reason for this fear is inexperience. Fund raisers new to major gift solicitation have great difficulty in accepting the fact that outright rejection is extremely rare. They see it as just a matter of time before anger and rejection combine into a very unpleasant experience. This fear is gradually overcome through experience as the fund raiser begins to understand that he or she and the prospective donor are bound together in a common bond—love of the institution or organization. This bond forges a team committed to pursuing common objectives for the benefit of the institution and, ultimately, for the accomplishment of its mission. As the fund raiser experiences the joy of working toward this common purpose, the fear subsides.

The nature of donor objections

Although the angry refusal is extremely rare (if not impossible), donors will not automatically agree to whatever you suggest. At times, they will make objections. And these objections typically arise in six areas:
1. focus of the gift;
2. timing of the gift;
3. size of the gift;
4. use of the gift;
5. administration of the gift; and
6. stewardship of the donor.

Focus of the gift. Many of the fund-raising profession's leading thinkers agree that one of the major issues of the 1990s is coordinating donors' desires with the priority needs of the institution. Often the donor's gift focus doesn't conform to the mission of the institution or to central elements of a capital campaign. Here, the donor's objection is straightforward and simply stated: "Your [institution's] need doesn't match my desire to help."

Consider Alicia Love, a wealthy agribusiness executive. She rose from very poor circumstances to her present position and lifestyle. When presented with a major gift proposal to support need-based scholarships at the university, she responds, "I worked two jobs to get through school and don't know why today's students can't do the same." As the major gift officer, you have two alternatives. You can push forward with the proposal and explain how today's students face greater obstacles and higher costs (perhaps you can persuade Ms. Love that the need outweighs her objection). Or you can try for a better understanding of her statement. You might respond, "Tell me how you earned your tuition and room and board." After learning about her experiences, you might respond, "Now I understand how you feel."

You might consider a follow-up response to Ms. Love: "What do you see as the most important issue to be confronted at the university?" Suppose she responds, "We need to focus the student on the priority issues in agriculture—the economics of farming." She has clarified her initial response as having to do with focus. She sees a more important need than the one you have proposed. You can now proceed to explore her needs and her readiness to support this perceived need for change of emphasis toward agricultural economics.

Timing of the gift. For most major gift asks, the timing of the gift is part of the proposal. For example, the requested amount might be "$300,000 paid over a three-year period." The donor might respond, "I would possibly consider that amount over five years," or "My company is just beginning to show an adequate profit. I couldn't begin a gift of that magnitude for another 18 months."

Do you push the timing issue? If so, how? If you respond, "We hope to wrap up the campaign in three years," you are giving a weak reason for gift timing.

If, however, you respond, "A gift over three years would allow us to begin recruitment of the faculty now," you've shifted the discussion from the institution's seemingly arbitrary deadline to a more justifiable basis for the request.

In any event, before you attempt to persuade the donor of the importance of the timing of the gift, you should seek to understand his or her needs. Then you can assess your ability to meet the request for a longer or delayed payment period.

Size of the gift. As with timing and focus, the requested amount of the gift needs to be rooted in clear and justifiable reasons as well as careful research into the donor's capacity to give. Suppose the request is for a $250,000 outright gift. You might say, "To establish a chair in dramatic arts would require $250,000. This amount would yield $12,500 annually to go to the chairholder as well as allow for a reasonable build-up of the endowment principal." Now, you and the donor have a wide range of alternative responses to pursue.

As we said earlier, there are no right words to use in asking for a major gift. This doesn't mean that there are no appropriate responses. For example, say you want to ask for a $500,000 gift. You might say, "We were wondering if you would consider a gift in the range of $500,000 to establish...." The key words are "consider" and "in the range" (yes, a single amount is not a range). Now the discussion is on consideration of an exploratory amount, and alternative responses are much broader than if you said, "Please give $500,000."

Use of the gift. A review of many major gift proposals will quickly reveal that more effort goes into explaining gift size and timing than detailing specifically how the gift will be used to address the opportunity being proposed.

When preparing the proposal, place yourself in the role of the donor. Have you given a clear and complete explanation of how the gift proceeds are to be used? Perhaps you should ask a colleague who is unfamiliar with the proposal to review it for clarity. After reviewing the proposal with the donor, don't rush past the explanation of how the gift is to be used. Patiently question the donor to assure yourself that he or she understands exactly how the gift will be employed to address the needs of the institution or organization.

Administration of the gift. When misunderstandings and objections arise *after* the gift has been agreed to, it is often because important issues regarding administration of the gift weren't properly addressed.

If the gift is outright, are there any gift-administration or cost-recovery fees charged by the institution? If securities are the basis of the gift, what is the date of valuation? What brokerage fees, if any, are assessed? Does the donor understand your institution's policy regarding immediate sale of all gifted securities? If real estate is involved, a multitude of issues must be addressed, including fees, tax obligations, title insurance, appraisals, and disposal of personal property.

All issues regarding administration should be addressed in the proposal. The donor will see that your institution is as careful in distributing the gift assets as he or she was in acquiring them.

Stewardship of the donor. A donor once lamented, "I got a lot of attention when I gave the gift, but I haven't heard any news regarding the gift since then." A broken promise or failure to follow through is the first step to a severed relationship with the donor.

What promises did you make about activities after the gift was made? Reports on student scholars' progress? A picture or tour of new facilities or equipment purchased? What about a periodic update regarding the funded research? If the proposal included a naming opportunity, was there follow-up? Was the naming exclusive to the donor or to be shared with other donors?

If an endowment is involved, is there an annual financial report? An annual activity report? Were parallel obligations of the institution carried out?

Chapter 7 discussed the 10 steps to success in major gift solicitation. The last step was to make a list of exit responsibilities—that is, you prepare a list of what you will do and what the donor will do. You should carefully review with the donor all understandings regarding the six areas underlying most donors' objections. Once you are in agreement, you should then ask, "If each of us satisfactorily carries out our obligations, then will you make the gift?"

Handling donor objections

In all six of these areas, as the above discussion indicates, the best way to handle donors' objections is to follow these four suggestions:
1. Seek to understand and clarify objections.
2. Be prepared to use alternative proposals.
3. Be flexible in your response.
4. Seek to maintain the relationship with the donor.

Seek to understand and clarify objections. Major gift officers often react to objections in different ways. Many seek to withdraw the proposal at the first sign of any objection. Some treat an objection as a signal to argue with the donor. Neither approach will produce positive results. Objections are a natural part of the major gift acquisition process. Donors have questions, opinions, and priorities. They aren't necessarily objecting when they challenge conclusions. Nor are they necessarily moving toward a rejection of the proposal when they object.

The first rule of handling objections is to return to information-seeking (see Chapter 11, Major Gift Solicitation: The Funnel Technique). Nothing is to be gained by attempting to move the donor toward agreement until you have clarified and understood his or her objections. For example, consider the following dialogue:

> **Donor:** I agree that Asian History is important, but probably not a $750,000 priority for the college.

> **Officer:** That's interesting. Tell me more about your concerns.

> **Donor:** Well, an endowed chair would be a welcome addition to the history department, but what about the fact that only 48 students are majoring in Asian History?

> **Officer:** The numbers are rising slightly each year. Are you suggesting a different emphasis?

Donor: Have you considered why more students aren't majoring in Asian History?

Officer: One of the problems is lack of adequate scholarships and fellowships.

Donor: What's adequate?

Officer: For an undergraduate scholarship, $10,000 would be competitive. A graduate fellowship of $15,000 would be required to attract top-flight graduate students. Did financial aid help you as an undergraduate?

Donor: I got the Salquist Scholarship in my senior year. It not only made it possible to finish in four years, but I could afford to marry Claudia. [Laughs.]

Officer: Was Claudia on a scholarship?

Donor: Definitely not. [Tells long story about the wealth on Claudia's side of the family.]

Officer: The other problem in attracting more majors is lack of sufficient faculty in Asian History. We have five, but need three more.

Donor: So an endowed chair will attract one new faculty member? How many students will be attracted?

Officer: A fund of $750,000 would earn $37,500 per year, and the principal would keep pace with inflation. If you chose to fund scholarships, at $10,000 per scholarship, almost four students per year would be helped.

Donor: How many students would be attracted to Asian Studies with an additional faculty member?

Officer: It's difficult to give an exact number, but we do know a good teacher can attract additional students and influence a lot of students' lives. [Earlier in the conversation] you mentioned Dr. Lee, our first chair-holder in Asian Studies. How did he influence you and Claudia?

Donor: [Tells a long affectionate story about Dr. Lee.]

By retreating from the proposal in order to understand and clarify the donor's objections, the major gift officer was able to learn more about his thinking about institutional priorities. The conversation opened up two avenues for support, and the ask amount of $750,000 is quantified in the donor's terms.

Hear an objection? Relax and listen to discover the root of the problem. Often you can't move forward without going backward first.

Be prepared to use alternative proposals. Let's assume you have systematically cultivated the prospect. You have done exhaustive research and are confident of your gift focus and the ask amount. Do you need to be prepared to consider alternative proposals? Absolutely!

As we discovered from the conversation above, the donor may not agree with either the gift focus or the ask amount. You should always be ready with the proverbial Plan B.

An alternative proposal may be no more than a slight variation of your original proposal, or it may be substantially different. You need to listen aggressively to the donor and be prepared to accommodate requested changes if they are mutually beneficial. While you cannot accept changes that move the scope or intent of the proposal outside the priorities of the institution, often the real issue is not the changes but your readiness to hear and accommodate the donor's needs. Consider this example:

Donor: I applaud the university for its desire to establish a department of Native American Studies. My people's history and achievements have long been ignored.

Officer: I am pleased that you are in favor of our proposal; this idea has been a long time coming.

Donor: Well, I certainly favor the intent of the proposal.

Officer: Oh. Tell me more.

Donor: We need to ensure that Native American students not only study our history, but that they move into the sciences, engineering, and medicine.

Officer: There is a real need there, but the number of Native Americans enrolled in the sciences is very small. Part of the reason for small numbers is that too few Native American students attend our university in the first place. How do we get more Native Americans to enroll?

Donor: [Gives lengthy discourse on increasing Native American enrollment through scholarships, a mentorship program, and incentives (summer employment) to pursue a degree in the sciences, engineering, and medicine.]

Officer: Great idea! I'd like to discuss this with our president and the deans and get back to you with a formal proposal for financial support.

Note that the institution and the donor have similar concerns, but different means to related ends. By being open to ideas that are not in the formal request, the matching gift officer maintains the relationship with the donor and moves in directions that are more central to the donor's priorities.

Be flexible in your response. Not only must you be open to alternative proposals (as in the conversation above), but you must also be flexible in your communicated responses. Responses will vary depending on your relationship with the donor and the stage of cultivation. For example, sometimes you might respond to a question with a question:

Donor: The global economy is undergoing a lot of change. Don't you agree?

Officer: Rapid change seems the norm in a lot of areas. What economic changes are of concern to you?

Not every statement made by the donor requires a response. You may choose purposeful silence (which, in itself, is a response):

Donor: Kids today don't understand the value of a good education.

Officer: [Silence.]

Donor: Hard work would make kids realize that money doesn't grow on trees.

Officer: Mmm.

Donor: Of course, working during the school years can mean it takes longer to graduate.

Officer: [Nods agreement.]

Donor: There is a problem.

Officer: [Responds accordingly.]

In this example, the donor is really thinking out loud, processing information, and not expecting or requiring a response.

In any conversation, we shift back and forth between information-seeking (questions and listening) and information-giving (talking). In conversation with a donor, it is critical to continually monitor the dialogue by aggressively listening to the donor and assessing what type of response is required.

Is the donor fully informed about the proposal? Should you test his or her knowledge with additional questions, or should you talk more, give more information? Have you moved into information-giving prematurely? Are you risking "losing" the donor? If you are to be successful, each of these questions needs to be addressed throughout the conversation.

Seek to maintain the relationship with the donor. In the pressure to meet campaign goals or annual major gift production goals, be careful that you don't lose sight of the need to maintain your relationship with the donor.

The gift proposal may not fit the interests of the donor. Sometimes the institution's needs may not correspond to the philanthropic objectives of the donor. Stated another way, the donor's desires may not be within the mission or priorities of the institution. In either case, it is better to recognize the mismatch and preserve the relationship than to attempt to force agreement.

Systematic cultivation and stewardship are a lifetime activity. The length, nature, and intensity of the relationship with the donor are the characteristics that distinguish major gift work from all other development activities.

Finally, remember that objections are a normal part of conversation. Understanding comes through a conversational exchange that includes objections. But an objection is *not* a rejection. The latter can be final—a dead end; the former is often only a bump in the road to agreement.

Note

[1] *The Chronicle of Higher Education,* September 11, 1991, A35.

Chapter 13

Major Gift Communication and Stewardship Through Group Cultivation Events

So far we have emphasized face-to-face communication with major gift prospects, but group cultivation events are also an important part of fund raising. While meeting with a prospect, you should seek opportunities to invite him or her to group cultivation events. Group events give the prospect the chance to visit your organization or institution and to meet others who support its mission. Group events are also an ideal way to provide stewardship to donors.

Just because a group event is less personal than a one-on-one meeting doesn't mean that you can be less concerned about the communication process. This could lead to a waste of opportunity and precious resources. Rather, consider group gatherings as a way to make many face-to-face contacts at the same time. The contact and stewardship process continues, but the setting and number of people change. One veteran major gift fund raiser calls this "partying with a purpose."

The mix of donors and prospects encourages natural conversation. Donors are often eager to share their story of why they decided to support your institution and to talk about what they are supporting. As peers, they can cultivate other prospects in a self-reinforcing communication. Prospects can ask questions and hear opinions that may not arise in conversation with a major gift officer.

Before you begin to plan a group cultivation event, you need to address two important questions: Where will you hold the event and how much will you spend on it?

The location question: Where will it be?

In an earlier chapter, we dealt with the importance of location in scheduling a one-on-one contact. Selecting location for a group event is equally important. The first choice for an event will almost always be the location of the institution or organization. Words become reality and vision takes form when donors and prospects see the nonprofit in action.

You can be innovative when choosing a location. This is especially true when you are visualizing how people can be motivated by their visit to the campus or organization site. For example, a lunch-box buffet in hard hats may serve as a theme to tour the expansion of your facilities. Or you might serve hors d'oeuvres in several places that guests must find with a map. In this way, donors and prospects provide their own self-guided tour of the facilities. Or consider offering food provided by students in a food preparation class. Guests who eat gourmet food as the young people explain their culinary techniques will take away a much deeper impression than if they had been sent a handful of glossy brochures on the same topic.

The second choice for a group event is the home of a volunteer. Many people enjoy entertaining groups in their home, and guests enjoy the intimacy that a private home offers. The "curiosity factor" cannot be ignored. People enjoy seeing how other people live, what decor they have chosen, and how they entertain. Using their homes to entertain institutional supporters and prospects is an important way for donors to make a contribution.

A public banquet facility at a club, hotel, or restaurant is usually the last choice. The impersonal surroundings offer limited opportunities for showcasing the institution and the importance of its mission.

Consider the location question carefully. Your choice forms the foundation for the rest of the planning.

The stewardship funding question: How much will it cost?

Deciding how much will be spent on a group cultivation event is a question of stewardship of funds. Both overspending and underspending reflect poor stewardship of the philanthropy of donors. Although you would plan your budget differently if the event itself were a fund raiser, you would still want to match fiscal prudence against marketing extravagance.

You would probably not have a wine and cheese party to celebrate a million-dollar gift or a black-tie gala to honor a $1,000 gift. Both gifts are important, but how you acknowledge them sends out significant signals to prospects and donors about how gifts translate into action.

It is tempting to deal with this question by repeating old solutions when dealing with spending levels of group events. But here is an opportunity to use ingenuity and innovation to reduce costs. For example, say a French-style, five-course dinner is $75 per person. How about changing the theme to a Spring Thanksgiving for Support and have a family-style meal? Here, the cost may be $25 per person. Is an old-fashioned box lunch raffle an option? Or a dinner of ethnic food prepared by people helped by your nonprofit?

Your organization's mission and its constitutency will provide ideas appropriate to your own situation. The important ingredient to containing event costs is to consider a wide range of options.

Another stewardship funding question you must confront is your choice of a gift to thank a major donor. Choosing a gift requires careful thought. Your decision on this point can enhance or destroy a relationship. Begin with your knowledge of the donor, his or her likes and dislikes, hobbies, and activities. Instead of an expensive but impersonal gift, try to select a gift that reflects the personality of the donor.

Examples of innovative acknowledgments include placing some memento of the donor in a time capsule during a cornerstone-setting ceremony, or producing a videotape of the recipients thanking the donor for services made possible by his or her gift. A framed photograph of the donor leading a groundbreaking ceremony with an antique tractor may be treasured far more than a plaque or trophy. Obtaining a personally autographed book by one of the donor's favorite authors shows thoughtfulness and care.

Your knowledge of your donors and your institution's mission and traditions should be fertile ground for appropriate ideas.

Planning a group cultivation event

It is rare to hold an event in which *something* doesn't go wrong, but careful planning, preparation, and follow-up can help keep the magnitude of the glitches to inconveniences rather than disasters. The steps outlined below can increase the likelihood that your event will go smoothly and be a success.

Step 1: Select the event. It is unfortunate but true that planning a group cultivation and stewardship event often begins with the attempt to reinvent the wheel. The major gift officer says, "Let's have an event," rather than asking, "Which of our upcoming events would serve a group cultivation and stewardship purpose?" The latter approach saves time and money and offers a better opportunity for connecting the prospect to the core activities of the organization.

For example, suppose you are the major gift officer at a large hospital. You would like to open the fall season with a group event. Instead of manufacturing your own special event, you inspect the calendar and find the following events already scheduled:

• dedication of the new Emergency Wing;
• opening of the expanded gift shop and volunteer center;
• an international symposium on "Providing Quality Medical Care for the Aged"; and
• celebration of the 1,000th flight of the LifeFlight Helicopter.

Each of these events offers a unique opportunity to showcase different aspects of the hospital's mission, and each one could serve a dual purpose. Piggybacking your own goals onto one of these events will probably make it more interesting in its focus and save the institution both money and time.

Step 2: Establish objectives. Often the planning process begins with only a vague idea of the purposes of the event. By forcing yourself to develop specific written objectives, you can improve the chances of meeting those objectives in the planning process. Objectives may include the following:

• *Introduction of major donors and prospects to each other.* This objective accomplishes two important elements of major gift fund raising by establishing in the minds of prospects (1) the successful nature of the institution or organization, and (2) the fact that their peers are supporters.

• *Continued cultivation of prospects.* Cultivation is a process, not a single event or series of unrelated events. The group gathering moves the cultivation along as a bridge between face-to-face contacts.

• *Stewardship.* This objective encompasses two purposes: publicly thanking a donor for his or her financial or volunteer support, and showing the donor and his or her friends the results of the contribution. Dollars are translated into action. The vision becomes reality, and all share in the joy of accomplishment.

• *Scheduling specific contacts.* Often a group event offers the only feasible opportunity to introduce specific donors to other donors, staff, or volunteers. For example, a prospect may express admiration for another prospect or donor. While it might be awkward to try to arrange a face-to-face contact, a group event enables the meeting to happen in a relaxed setting. In addition, a group event enables the nonprofit's president or CEO and key volunteers to meet and socialize with many prospects.

• *Internal cultivation.* Don't forget that your internal audience needs as much cultivation as external audiences. Since the organization's goals are tied to outcomes related to external happenings (number of gifts received, total gift income, number of contacts made), fund raisers naturally tend to focus on this area. But goals related to the external support network would be very difficult to achieve if the staff and administration did not understand and appreciate how both audiences depend on each other.

Make internal cultivation a part of every event. You need to demonstrate that investing budget dollars in external relations is a wise choice. You can do this by involving key staff and administrators with donors and prospects. Each person should be given specific assignments (as discussed below) and appropriate recognition when positive outcomes occur. A skeptic soon becomes a believer when he or she is part of securing a major gift.

• *Establishment of evaluation measurements.* Was the gathering successful? Did it achieve your goals? Obviously there is no way to evaluate unless you have established objectives and measurements. For example, one of your goals may be to "put on a first-class event." This goal is meaningless without a specific definition of "first class" and a way to measure whether you have achieved it. You need to consider such things as setting specific budget targets, establishing invitation acceptance levels by particular invitees, and achieving other preestablished objectives. Success at what cost? Cultivation of whom? You can only evaluate outcomes if you have established specific criteria of success.

In Scotland, people are fond of recalling the time a tourist stopped an old farmer to inquire how to get to a certain town. The farmer thought a moment, then replied, "Well, I wouldn't start out from *here*." The farmer and the tourist may have agreed on the objective, but they disagreed on the criteria for measuring success.

Step 3: Establish the invitation list. Your invitation list should flow from your objectives. If, for example, the objective is stewardship of Mr. and Ms.

Smith's gift to create a lakeside camp for inner-city children, then you know that the Smiths are the "stars" of the evening, and the gift is the focus of the program. The invitation list follows from these facts.

You should have a reason for including every person on the invitation list. In the midst of a busy day it may be difficult to concentrate on creating an invitation list for an event six weeks in the future, but don't yield to the temptation to invite "the same old gang." You will be wasting both money and opportunity. You can create a better list by adding more names than you intend to invite and then eliminating the necessary number according to an agreed-upon priority or criterion.

Involve volunteers in creating the invitation list. First show them the written objectives, and then ask them whom they would invite. Ask for their permission to add a note to the invitation stating "Invitation sent at the request of [volunteer's name]." Ask staff to make suggestions. If the purpose of the event is to honor someone, this person should be encouraged to furnish a list of a specific number of invitees.

Many nonprofits are stuck with events that have a long tradition that dictates invitees and program. If you feel the focus of the event or the list of invitees needs changing, involve others in the decision. Change is difficult, changing tradition almost impossible. But, if after wide consultation, you determine that changes are required, you must move boldly. If the changes are sweeping, you may wish to take incremental steps or announce that the changed event is a one-time test.

Step 4: Establish the form of the invitation. Another mistake is to breathe a sigh of relief when the invitation list is complete and say, "Let's get these in the mail." Remember that every invitation offers another opportunity for creative communication. You need to consider each prospect's name and ask, "How can I maximize this cultivation opportunity?"

Consider these possibilities for enhancing the communication impact of a written invitation:

• Include with the formal invitation a handwritten note from the CEO, a key volunteer, or a friend of the prospect. The note conveys the writer's hope that the recipient will attend the event.

• Send a letter before the formal invitations are mailed. The letter, which can be personalized as appropriate, informs the prospect of the date and time of the event and says that "an invitation will follow."

• Telephone the prospect a day or so after he or she has received the invitation. This conveys the message that the prospect's attendance is really important. The phone call is also useful if you want to inform the prospect that he or she will be seated in a place of honor or at a certain table. Another approach is to call the prospect two days before the event to tell him or her of the proposed seating arrangements. Some prospects appreciate receiving a list of other guests that describes each person's role at the institution or organization.

• Call guests or send them a short note after the event to express your appreciation for their attendance.

The invitation process offers a unique opportunity for one-on-one contact with the prospect and for reinforcing your message that he or she is important to the organization or institution.

Step 5: Make cultivation assignments. If practical, give every staff member, administrator, and key volunteer cultivation assignments before the event. This reinforces the message that there is a purpose to the expenditure of time and money. Everyone feels a more important part of the event if he or she has a specific set of duties to achieve. Begin by reviewing your objectives and invitation list. Establish priority assignments and peer groupings. From this process your assignments will begin to take shape.

First, however, consider two caveats: The assignments of cultivation contacts need to be done by those most familiar with the people involved. If possible, those making the contacts should be involved in making the specific assignments. This is not something that you can assign to a member of the clerical staff. Second, each assignment must be agreed to by the person who will be making the contact. You should phone or visit each volunteer to determine his or her "comfort level" with the assignment and to remind the volunteer to prepare a debriefing memo after the contact. Since you are involving volunteers in this process, you need to remember that they, too, have been cultivated in this manner.

Let's assume that you are the major gift officer for the Springdale Philharmonic Orchestra Foundation. The opening night cocktail and buffet is planned, and you have prepared four assignments for the CEO of the foundation. Each assignment is placed on a 3x5 card as follows:

STRICTLY CONFIDENTIAL

PRESIDENT'S CULTIVATION ASSIGNMENT

Donors: Robert "Bob" Treut
Elaine "E.B." Cheever
Kansas City, Missouri

History: Married couple. He is owner/CEO of Treut Engineering. She is a physician—Family Practice Clinic. Each is a member of the Founder's Council.

Giving History: Since 1985: $148,000. Last gift, 2/1/94, $25,000 to underwrite addition of "green room."

Assignment:

1. Thank them for gift. You've sent letter of thanks.

2. Note Bob was just elected president of Chamber of Commerce.

3. Note E.B. recovering from back surgery.

4. Invite them to post-concert dessert.

Note: Debriefing memos due to Research Office within two days.

Give out the assignment cards before the event—the day before or early on the day of the event. Many development officers carry two sets of assignment cards for *all* assignments. One set is for monitoring purposes, and the other is a replacement in case any of the volunteers lose or forget theirs.

Step 6: Assign cultivation liaison. The president or CEO, board chair, or key volunteers may need to have a person assigned to them to facilitate contacts. You may need to perform this function yourself for the president or CEO. You would accompany the CEO or president at the event to introduce donors and prospects and to remind him or her of names and important facts as the two of you "work the room." For example, when you encounter newer donors, you can avoid embarrassment by saying, "Chancellor, you know the Crawfords. Bob and Eloise. Eloise, how did the Docents' meeting go? Bob, is it true that you are really thinking of retirement and a trip to Paris?" The chancellor is at ease. The Crawfords are flattered that the chancellor demonstrates personal interest in them. You are helping to achieve one of the agreed-upon objectives.

One way to judge how well a cultivation event is going is to watch how groups are forming during the event. If the staff groups together, a failure is imminent. If the new donors are standing separate from the established volunteer leadership, failure is assured. If the CEO is standing alone, failure on all counts is in the works. If, on the other hand, everyone is having a good time (top priority) and doing their cultivation assignments (second priority), then you've achieved success in this important step.

A staff assignment list may be briefer since their knowledge of the prospects is probably more extensive than that of administration or key volunteers. Your assignment sheet is, in essence, a reminder or "to do" list. It may look like the following:

STRICTLY CONFIDENTIAL

PRE-EVENT CULTIVATION ASSIGNMENTS

1. Introduce Mike and "Berry" Standard to President Jackson.

2. Ask Richard and Shirley Boysten if meeting regarding Cancer Center Endowment Fund can be set in next two weeks.

3. Invite Rachel White to join London Theater Trip.

4. Thank "Sissy" Sisson for gift of Laser Lab.

5. Make sure President Jackson publicly toasts Henry Black's agreement to provide a leadership gift of $50,000 to Hospice Center. Note: Black does not want to speak, but Dr. Flaherty will respond on behalf of Center.

Step 7: Make preliminary seating assignments. As we all know the truth of that cliche of our profession, "People give to people—peers give to peers," the importance of this step will be evident. Possibly the most important element in planning a successful cultivation event is creating the seating plan that maximizes the opportunity for guests to enjoy one another's company.

This step should begin with reviewing the event's objectives and developing a seating plan in accordance with those objectives. A seating plan conveys status and honors the guests' contribution of time, talent, and financial resources. For this reason, great sensitivity is necessary to make sure that the correct "messages" are sent. Begin by assigning a host to each table. The host (whether staff or volunteer) should clearly understand that it is his or her responsibility to introduce people and to monitor the flow of conversation so that one person doesn't dominate while others are ignored.

Location of the seating is second in importance to the individual's seating assignment. It also sends a message. One major gift fund raiser wanted to have a head table for 20 people at an event planned for 65 people. Because this would mean that almost a third of the guests were at the head table, she decided to do away completely with the head table. Instead she assigned two of the "head table" people as hosts at each of 10 tables. These head table VIPs wore a rosebud and blue ribbon. At the time of introductions, the head table hosts were identified, but all the tables were equally important.

If you are unsure of a particular seating arrangement, take the time to check it out. For example, you could call one of the couples and inform them of the proposed seating and then ask, "How do you feel about the grouping?" If there are problems, you will probably hear about them at that time.

Remember that the seating chart is subject to change up until the time people are seated. Cancellations and additions are the bane of an event-planner's existence, but they cannot be avoided, and they must be handled with care. Ill-advised, last-minute shuffling of seating assignments can undo your entire plan.

Step 8: Plan media coverage. Like most of the previous steps, this step begins with a review of overall event objectives. Media coverage is planned to enhance those objectives.

Consider the basic questions: First of all, do you *want* any coverage? Perhaps you feel that media coverage will detract from the major objectives and destroy the free flow of conversation. If, on the other hand, you decide that coverage is desirable, what should the focus be? Social? Service? Serious? Your answer to this question will help you determine whether the event should be covered by the society press or the news media.

If media coverage is part of the plan, you need to send out a media advisory/press release in advance of the gathering. Canvassing the newspaper and television assignment editors on the day of the event will give you an idea of the volume and type of coverage you can expect.

As you are planning media coverage, be aware of two basic realities: First, freedom of the press means that the press will cover what they want in whatever manner they choose. You are always taking a risk when you invite media coverage. The value of exposing your institution's mission to a wider audience must be offset by the possibility of unforeseen negative reporting. For example, what you see as a social occasion may be reported as a personality profile of one of the guests. Reporters may ignore the program purpose in favor of observations of the guests on a topic far afield from the intended purpose of the event.

As a courtesy to your guests, always assign a staff member to accompany members of the press. Guests should be aware that they are speaking "on the record" to the press. The staff member should not interfere with the free interchange of ideas or conversation; his or her role is to make the guests aware that their conversation is not an intimate one-on-one aside.

The second reality is that your own internal communications staff will also expect to enjoy freedom of the press in the selection of story focus and coverage options. Your priority may be a picture and story of the donor presenting her check to your institution, but communication people tend to have great disdain for what they call "gab and grab" or "cocktails and conversation" story opportunities. They argue that it is poor journalism. Perhaps they are correct.

The best way to deal with this second reality is to work with the communications staff to achieve both objectives. Perhaps a feature interview with the donor will satisfy their desire for good journalism and your objective of acknowledging the gift to your institution. Even better would be a story on the gift focus and why the donor chose this area to support.

Press photojournalists offer another opportunity to achieve your objectives if you do advance planning. You need to determine the individuals or groups whose pictures you would like to include in the coverage of the event. Then give this list to the photographer as you escort him or her to those people.

Establish the limits of television coverage in advance. Since lights and cameras can be intrusive, you need to decide how much of the event will be open for coverage. When outside speakers or performers are involved, you need to ask their permission if you plan to have television coverage. This will avoid possible embarrassment and misunderstandings during the event.

As you plan media coverage, ask yourself, "Am I thinking of the best interests of the donors and prospects?" This guideline will help you make decisions about media coverage for a wide range of situations.

Step 9: Assign event management roles. In order for your event to be successful, you need to distinguish between the roles of two key people—that of the overall event manager (usually the special events person on the staff) and the guest manager (usually the major gift officer).

The overall event manager is in charge of everything except the cultivation and communication with the guests. The event manager takes part in all decisions, including location, program, invitations, seating, entertainment, and food and drink. Once these decisions are made, the event manager implements and executes them. During the event itself, the event manager is the person "in charge," and he or she should deal with all "non-people" problems.

The guest manager sees that cultivation assignments are being carried out and handles all problems dealing with the care and comfort of the guests.

Distinguishing between these two roles will avoid the after-event lament, "I was so busy I didn't get to talk to anyone." If the event manager makes that complaint, there is no need for concern. That's the nature of this particular assignment. But if the complaint is made by the guest manager, then the event has failed in one of its basic purposes.

Some overlapping of roles is bound to happen. Last-minute seating changes usually involve both managers. These crises can be reduced, if not eliminated, by careful planning. As in your own home, the enjoyment of your guests and their "care and feeding" is your first concern. You have a dual responsibility here—you are working, but you are also relaxing (believe it or not!). Both can be achieved when you follow these nine steps of pre-event planning.

Post-event steps

In a very real sense, as you probably already know only too well, no job having to do with donor cultivation is ever really "over." Once an event has ended, there are four essential follow-up steps.

Step 1: Debrief the event. Two or three days after the event, your opinions have solidified on how well it achieved your objectives. Before you hold an evaluation meeting for everyone who was involved in planning the event, ask each person to consult trusted volunteers for their reactions. At the evaluation meeting, review each objective and determine how to improve the success rate at future events. If an objective was not achieved, perhaps the objective itself was impractical, poorly stated, or inappropriate. These issues need to be addressed honestly by people who feel as free to confront failure as they are to celebrate success.

Conclude this step by preparing a written evaluation. This document will serve as the basis for planning the next event of similar character and objectives.

Step 2: Secure research. Within 48 hours, each person with a cultivation assignment should have prepared debriefing memos regarding his or her particular assignment. These memos are incorporated into the existing donor/prospect research files. (As mentioned above, it's important to consider cautions regarding ethical conduct as knowledge of the donor/prospect is translated into a written document.)

Step 3: Prepare thank-you letters. Within three days after the event, you should have conveyed your thanks to everyone who attended. There are several ways of doing this:

- a formal thank-you card;
- a letter;
- a handwritten note; or
- a telephone call.

As you prepare your thank-you's, don't forget your internal audience. Their time is valuable too, and they should be thanked for helping to make the event a success.

Step 4: Record attendance. You need to use a system to record the attendance of each guest in a database for future reference. This record will serve as a basis for future invitation lists. The software required for this program is commonplace and can be handled as a lower staff priority. Your ability to retrieve the data for each guest—name, address, phone number, and any special needs, such as wheelchair use or food preferences—will save valuable time and effort as you plan future events.

Group cultivation events are an important part of the process of establishing long-term relationships with your prospective major gift donors. They present one of the best opportunities to validate the mission of the institution or organization you represent. Your care in planning this opportunity will further demonstrate your concern and professionalism.

Chapter 14

Taking a Step Back

A s we said in the preface, the purpose of this book is "to explore various strategies for major gift solicitation." The hypothesis was that carefully planned preparation for each phase of the solicitation process would help ensure a successful outcome.

Major decision points and conclusions

As you have proceeded through this book, the chapters have presented these major decision points and conclusions:

1. As the major gift officer you will succeed only if your organization or institution has structured itself to allow ongoing face-to-face cultivation and solicitation to take place.

2. Fears and myths surrounding major gift solicitation can keep you from contacting prospects. But facing the fears and dispelling the myths can enable you to grow in confidence and to experience the joy that philanthropy brings to all parties.

3. Understanding how you communicate and how others respond will give you the confidence to cultivate and solicit major gifts face-to-face.

4. Understanding the major gift "ask"—from making the appointment to closing the meeting—will free you from worrying about the mechanics of the meeting so that you can concentrate on the needs and desires of the prospects.

Understanding each of these very important conclusions can make you more effective as a major gift fund raiser. But it's also important that you don't get so involved in examining the trees that you fail to see the forest. Talk to any experienced major gift officer about his or her job, and you will never hear stories about the strategies and mechanics of orchestrating a solicitation. Instead, you will hear enthusiastic tales of relationships built, dreams realized, and donors joyfully involved in the life of the institution.

Joyful matchmaking

We are in the business of "matchmaking," as Virginia Kelsch, associate vice chancellor for university relations at the University of California, Davis, calls it. We seek to understand the needs and desires of the donors. Once we have a clear picture of the donor's wishes, we look for a match in keeping with the mission and priority needs of our institution.

Matchmaking is a joyful enterprise! You are helping your donors discover that what is important to them is also important to your independent school, college, or university. Their values, their opinions are shared and "institutionalized." When a gift results from this shared purpose, the community discovers a marriage of aspirations, and what was essentially a private matter between the institution and the donor can now be revealed to its internal and external constituencies. People who hear about the gift and its purpose are then motivated to consider their own philanthropic plan.

After the announcement of a major gift, it is very common for people to telephone the institution and express their wish to discuss a similar gift. Publicity serves as a beacon to guide and motivate others to give.

The result? A positive philanthropic climate or "ethos" develops, and with nurturing and encouragement it widens to encompass an increasing circle of donors and prospects. And you are in the center of this circle, focusing on the real purpose of your job as major gift officer: to help other people achieve their goals. As someone once observed, "Philanthropy [becomes] the mystical mingling of a joyous giver, an artful asker, and a grateful recipient."[1]

Note

[1] Douglas M. Lawson, fund-raising consultant and author of *Give to Live: How Giving Can Change Your Life* (La Jolla, CA: Alti Publishing, 1991).

Section 2:

Case Studies

Section 1 dealt with communication in face-to-face solicitation of major gifts. Section 2 contains 11 case studies designed to enable you to apply your knowledge of solicitation techniques in developing strategies for securing major gifts. Each case varies as to gift purpose and size, type of organization or institution, background of prospective donor, and background and experience of the development officer.

You can obtain maximum benefit from your study of each case by following the procedure below:

1. Read the case quickly.

2. Reread the case carefully and mark the important points.

3. Answer each question based upon your experience and background and what you have learned from this book. There is no single "right" answer.

4. Ask a colleague to do steps 1-3. Confer and compare your strategies before you turn to the discussion in Section 3.

5. The discussion does not provide specific answers, because there is no one best solution. This section suggests possible strategies and alternatives as a way to stimulate further thinking.

These cases contain fictional organizations and institutions, people, and situations. Although they are based, in part, on composites of actual situations, any direct resemblance to real people, situations, organizations, or institutions is purely coincidental.

James Knox College

J ames Knox College will soon celebrate its 100-year anniversary. A centennial celebration will begin in nine months. Plans are well underway
to use the anniversary to reach out to alumni, friends, and the community.
As President Edward Deeble said, "It is time that Knox reaffirmed the
partnerships that built this college and helped to move it into the educational
leadership position it now enjoys."

In 1894, one could hardly have forecast an institution that is regarded by
the *Borden's College Guide* as "one of the West's best-kept secrets as a quality
liberal arts college." The college was established by James Knox, a Presbyterian missionary/preacher. He saw the purpose of the college as "to train
up Christian young men and women to make meaningful contributions to
the church and society." Starting with 45 students in three residential buildings,
the college grew slowly but steadily in the early 1900s.

The Depression took its toll on Knox. The board of trustees twice considered closing the doors. Each time, last-minute gifts returned the college
to financial solvency. As Michael Standard, Class of '31, says, "We knew that Knox
would survive even when we weren't sure where our next meal was coming from."

The post-World War II period provided a great influx of students. Enrollment grew to 675 students. The 325-acre campus was the site of a continuous
building program. The adjoining community, Millvale, enjoyed similar prosperity.

Knox College has 2,150 full-time undergraduates. Its 124 faculty members
consider themselves teachers rather than researchers. The curriculum remains
focused on liberal arts, teaching, and extended learning programs. The faculty
take great pride in being known as "people who still care about the individual."
Students are regularly invited to professors' homes for discussion and social activities.

Rising tuition costs plague the administration, and building maintenance
is deferred regularly. Nevertheless, the board of trustees has managed to
balance the budget without borrowing from the $31 million endowment fund.

A year-long academic planning process has established need-based scholarships as the institution's top priority. This need has been widely communicated to the Knox alumni and friends.

Knox is healthy in most respects. Enrollment grows by about 15 to 20 students a year. Student retention is 81 percent. The community of Millvale (population 185,000) takes pride in "its hometown college."

Prospective donors

Everyone says that Bob and Abby Rogers are living proof that opposites attract. He is confident and extroverted, one of Millvale's "movers and shakers." Abby is quiet, avoids the limelight, and leaves no doubt that she is content to let Bob take the lead.

Knox College has always played a key role in the Rogers family. Abby's parents both graduated from Knox. Bob and Abby met at Knox in their sophomore year. The two Rogers children, Katy and Steve, attended Knox. Bob boasts that his family "could field a basketball team of loyal Knox alumni."

Although Bob seems to be active in everything in the community, Knox College remains at the center of his concerns. This spring he will celebrate 25 years of service on the Knox board of trustees. For the past three years, he has served as chair of the trustees

Bob divides his time between running a chain of successful furniture stores, known as Whiting's Furniture Shops, and helping daughter Katy in her efforts to start a gourmet food takeout restaurant. All indications are that Katy has "her dad's head for business."

Abby is active in the Greenview Presbyterian Church and serves as treasurer of the Board of Deacons. Pastor Richard Holden says, "Abby keeps us all out of trouble with her head for numbers. It seems she is always explaining the financial balance sheet to me."

Abby is seen occasionally at the furniture stores, but whether she has any specific role there is unknown.

Development officer

Bill Mathews has been vice president for development at Knox for 18 months. He enjoys an excellent reputation based on his 12 years in fund raising at two other small liberal arts colleges.

Bill enjoys a close relationship with President Ed Deeble. The president has often remarked that "hiring Bill Mathews was one of the smartest moves we've made in the 11 years I've been here." The rapport between the two of them is evident. Bill attributes Knox's tenfold increase in gift income over the past eight years to Deeble's leadership. The president's role in securing major gifts from older alumni is legendary. Although he is modest about his achievements, it is obvious that he is comfortable in the external relations role.

Mathews is pleased that gift income was up 21 percent last year, but he is concerned with the progress so far on the Centennial Campaign. The campaign was planned prior to his arrival. A consultant hired to evaluate the feasibility of the campaign expressed "cautious optimism that a campaign goal of $15 million is achievable with strong leadership and aggressive support by the board of trustees." Six months into the "Leadership Phase" of this campaign has resulted in five gifts totaling $800,000.

Bill Mathews is regarded as "the new boy" by Bob Rogers. He doesn't know Mathews well, but is pleased with the results he's seen. President Deeble's strong endorsement of Mathews is a significant factor in molding Rogers's opinion of Mathews and his progress.

Research background

Accumulated research on the Rogers family has resulted in a file two inches thick. It is filled with write-ups of previous visits, press clippings of Bob receiving the Knox Medal from the college, and news about Bob's other civic activities in the Millvale community. There is little information on Abby beyond a record of the times she's accompanied Bob in his visits to campus functions.

The Rogers' giving record is impressive for its length and continuous growth. Bob and Abby have made annual gifts every year since 1951. Their accumulated annual giving is $611,793. The annual gifts for the last three years have been $25,000, $27,500, and $30,000.

The Rogers have made three larger gifts in addition to their annual pledge. In 1968, they gave $50,000 to endow a sports scholarship to honor Abby's father. The Whitey Award is given annually to the athlete "who displays courage and skill on the field and leadership on the campus." In 1980, they gave $325,000 to remodel the library. The Rogers Wing houses the student study area. In 1988, they gave $100,000 to establish the President's Opportunity Fund.

A recent note in the file from President Deeble states, "Bob Rogers says he is thinking of retirement, but complains that son Steve doesn't have the family zeal for furniture merchandising." Deeble notes that Bob doesn't look forward to the "idleness of retirement." Conversation with other trustees confirms that Bob would retire if he could settle the future leadership of the furniture chain.

Major gift focus

President Deeble has conferred numerous times with Bill Mathews about "approaching Bob for a big gift to give the campaign a needed jolt." They agree that the focus should be student scholarships.

A proposal for a need-based Rogers Family Scholarship Fund is prepared. The proposal is complete except for a decision on the gift level. Deeble thinks "$500,000 sounds about right." Mathews argues that "now is the time to suggest $1 million and to ask Bob to chair the public phase of the campaign."

Assignment

You are Bill Mathews, and you and President Deeble agree that it would be worthwhile for you to "feel Bob out" about his campaign gift. Your objective is to "explore gift alternatives." As you prepare for this visit, consider how you would answer the following questions.

Prepare your answers in writing. Then, if possible, discuss your strategy with a colleague who has also read the case and prepared written answers. Together turn to Section 3 and read the discussion of Case A, beginning on page 149.

1. What do you think about the overall objective and meeting strategy? What alternatives would you suggest?

2. What key areas of discussion would reveal frame of reference and mental set?

3. What information needs to be obtained that isn't revealed in existing research?

4. What should your objectives be?

5. Where should the meeting be held?

6. Who should be included?

7. How should the question of gift focus be approached?

8. How should the question of gift level be approached?

9. Once you have answers to the above questions, what follow-up questions would you ask?

10. At this stage, how would you evaluate Knox College's prospects for obtaining a $1 million gift from the Rogers?

The Children's Alternatives Center

T he Children's Alternatives Center (CAC) was founded in 1948 by Jacob Elwin Nosek. His purpose was "to offer to the disadvantaged young people of Chicago the same opportunities enjoyed by youth throughout America."

Nosek embodied the Horatio Alger rise from poverty to riches. His parents immigrated from Poland in 1910. His father worked as a handyman along Chicago's "Gold Coast." People often said, "If it can be fixed, Nosek will fix it." Jacob's parents were strict disciplinarians who insisted that he study and excel in school. Although learning came easily for him, Jacob shared his father's fascination with mechanical objects. His aptitude for taking apart kitchen appliances and putting them back together brought pride to his parents and immense satisfaction to himself. Finally, college plans were set aside because of lack of finances and Jacob's insistence that he "make it on his own."

Make it he did! Working in the back of his father's shop, he developed many improvements in kitchen appliances. Through hard work, a lot of good luck, and financial backing provided by patents he obtained from modernizing the food mixer, Jacob built the leading appliance manufacturing concern in the United States. Kitchen Ease Corporation became a household word.

After World War II, Jacob became increasingly committed to finding a way to give back to society some of the financial resources he had accumulated. His search ended in 1950 with the founding grant of $250,000 to the Children's Alternatives Center. Until his death in 1982 at the age of 79, Jacob Nosek gave vigorous leadership to the CAC. He worked hard to keep the organization true to its founding purpose of helping Chicago's disadvantaged children through:

- contact with positive adult role models;
- creation of a healthy environment to develop good social skills; and
- tutorial assistance to develop and maintain strong learning skills.

In many ways, the CAC was a forerunner of today's concept of a model day-care center. Jacob often faced strong resistance from some members of

CAC's board, who claimed that he was ignoring other important needs of the financially impoverished young people of Chicago. But Jacob responded, "We cannot abandon our purpose to accommodate the fads of today."

At his death, Jacob left a bequest of $3 million to establish an endowment fund to "help meet the programmatic expenses associated with the CAC's founding purposes." The CAC has prospered in its 44 years of operation.

Janet Stratton, the president of the CAC, is known throughout the U.S. for her skillful leadership. Since assuming the presidency in 1975, Janet has built an excellent staff of 26 energetic advocates for the mission of the CAC. The major program components include:

- a preschool (ages 3 to 5) operated by staff and parents;
- an after-school learning enhancement center for ages 5 to 11, staffed by certified teachers and volunteer "grandmothers";
- a Games and Skills Center for ages 5-11 and 11-13, operated by physical education teachers, staff, and "brother-buddies";
- an educational assessment center for ages 6-11, staffed by professional testing technicians, parents, and volunteers.

Resources have always been tight for the CAC. There have always been more children with needs than staff or financial resources to service them. Stratton pioneered the concept of mixing professional staff and volunteers as direct service providers. The CAC Grandmothers program has been imitated by social service agencies throughout the U.S.

This program began because many women over 55 were eager to help the CAC. Stratton describes these volunteers as having "willing hands, energetic hearts, and little formal education." What most of them did have, however, was experience: They knew how to raise children. CAC organized classes to train these volunteers to help the certified teachers in CAC's various programs. The women who completed the training became CAC Grandmothers.

The CAC Brother-Buddies program was the idea of Michael Nosek, Jacob's son and board chair for Kitchen Ease Corporation. Nosek had observed a lot of wasted energy among the area's 17- to 19-year-old male population, and he believed that they could make a valuable contribution to the CAC Games and Skills Center if they were given the chance. He pushed hard to set up a comprehensive screening and training center to teach young men the skills necessary to be aides to CAC's physical education teacher. Today the CAC Brother-Buddies jacket is a prized possession among the area's older teens, and a Sister-Buddies program is in the planning stages.

The CAC physical education program works on building self-esteem and social skills. "Winning isn't even on our priority list," Michael explains, and he points out with pride that teams are never selected on the basis of skills, and that scoring is often ignored. CAC genuinely believes that the game is learning, not winning.

Even with such innovations in stretching the staffing dollar with volunteers, the budget remains tight. Stratton observes, "The Children's Alternatives Center can maintain itself with continued strong dedication of staff and the financial support of our many friends. But if we are to take any bold, new steps, a major infusion of capital is necessary."

Prospective donors

Everyone agrees that the only thing Michael Nosek and his sister Susan have in common is their parents. At 63 Michael is almost a carbon copy of his dad. He is considered to be a mechanical genius. At his father's death, he reorganized and modernized plant operations. Profits rose by more than 20 percent a year over the next 10 years. But with the recession of the early 1980s, costs rose, profits shrank, and credit infusions helped only marginally.

At 57 Susan Nosek is quite different from her brother. Although she claims to have "a limited understanding of the maufacturing side," she is widely recognized and sought after for her financial acumen. She is a highly skilled manager. As president and chief financial officer of Kitchen Ease, she is credited with rescuing the corporation from near-bankruptcy. The recent listing of Kitchen Ease at 271 in the Fortune 500 is a reversal hailed as the turnaround story of the 1990s.

Because Michael and Susan are so different in their interests and approaches, everyone is amazed at how effectively they work together as a team at Kitchen Ease. Open disagreement is rare. The Nosek children know their own strengths and weaknesses and defer to each other's expertise. This is, no doubt, the result of the strong family bond instilled in them by their parents—the Nosek family worked together and played together. "Family first" was Jacob and Emilie Nosek's motto. They were prouder of their children's teamwork than their successful careers. Although Michael was bright and energetic, he was an indifferent student. He attended the University of Illinois at the insistence of his parents. He sums up his college experience by joking, "I majored in football, minored in engineering, and graduated just in time to beat Susan through commencement." After graduation he returned home to join Kitchen Ease as an assistant in the design department.

Susan, on the other hand, was a brilliant student. She received her bachelor's degree from the University of Chicago and an M.B.A. from Harvard Business School. After graduation she spent four years in New York as a management consultant, and a year in Washington as a White House Fellow. She then returned home to begin work in the finance department at Kichen Ease.

Development officer

Kathy James, often called the "Renaissance Woman" of the CAC, was born and raised in Santa Cruz, California. She graduated from Stanford in Literature and Dramatic Arts. Self-taught on the cello, she became a serious music student after college. Kathy now plays with the Chicago Philharmonic.

To finance her interest in the arts, five years ago she began working as a publications/public relations assistant at CAC. Although she is a skilled writer and has a keen understanding of graphic arts, her forte is one-on-one personal communication. That Kathy cares deeply about CAC's mission is obvious in even the most mundane conversation about day-to-day activities.

Two years ago, Janet Stratton asked Kathy if she would consider assuming the recently vacated major gift development officer's post on an acting basis.

Within six months it was obvious to Janet and the CAC board that Kathy was a born fund raiser. She has developed a good rapport with most of the CAC major donor support base. She also has an excellent relationship with both Michael and Susan Nosek. Although personally she agrees with Susan's progressive views rather than Michael's more conservative approach to the CAC mission, Kathy is careful to keep her opinions separate from her professional duties.

Research background

"There are few secrets in running a publicly held corporation," laments Susan Nosek. "Your whole life is hung out for everyone to view," concurs Michael. For 55 years Kitchen Ease was a privately held concern. Two years ago, the Noseks took Kitchen Ease public, selling 58 percent of the stock at an opening price of $26/share. Today, the price is $43/share and climbing slowly and steadily.

According to the *Wall Street Investor,* "Kitchen Ease has gone public and avoided the urge to grow rapidly. Instead, CFO Susan Nosek has urged the corporation's board to invest in R&D. As a result, Kitchen Ease seems poised to be a technological leader for the next five- to 10-year period."

Both Susan and Michael have committed themselves to another five years at their present posts at Kitchen Ease. The corporation prospectus lists their annual salaries at $495,000 and $510,000 respectively. Stock holdings, including exercised stock options are as follows: Michael Nosek—1,238,000 shares, and Susan Nosek—1,511,000 shares.

Susan recently remarked to President Stratton that she and Michael want to complete their obligations to establish an endowment for CAC while they are still able to enjoy the fruits of their labors. Susan said that she and her brother have agreed to "do something significant" and to do it as soon as they can agree on the focus of their gift.

The Noseks are quite open in saying that a family trust set up by their father has provided for the future of their families. At their deaths, their Kitchen Ease stock will transfer to the family foundation trust. At the present time, their stock is held in separate trusts.

Major gift focus

Susan's remark regarding the need to bring focus to a major gift understates the case. She believes that times have changed, but the CAC "hasn't been allowed to change with the people it serves." She has long urged a study of the CAC mission to "bring it into focus with the 1990s." She is particularly concerned about the high dropout rate of the area's young people at the early high school level. The lack of dialogue between the student, parent, and teacher is especially troublesome to Susan. The CAC board is sympathetic, but feels that this is a "family fight that needs to be settled within the Nosek clan."

Michael is equally adamant that "the original vision of Jacob Nosek be retained." He remarked recently to Kathy James, "Dad's principles served us well in the last 50 years, and they'll serve us well in the next 50." Michael remains concerned with CAC's physical education program. His idea of relaxation is to "mix it up" with the CAC boys and girls on the basketball court.

Assignment

You are Kathy James. You and President Stratton would like to propose a major capital campaign to the CAC board of directors, but realize that such a proposal will be set aside until the Nosek Endowment question is settled. You and Stratton agree that both of you should visit the Noseks to "find a solution to our problem." Now consider the questions below.

Prepare your answers in writing. Then, if possible, discuss your strategy with a colleague who has also read the case and prepared written answers. Together turn to Section 3 and read the discussion of Case B, beginning on page 151.

1. Should you and Janet Stratton meet with the Noseks together or separately? What are the advantages and disadvantages of separate meetings?

2. Do you have enough facts to establish a set of meeting objectives? If so, what would those objectives emphasize?

3. Is gift focus the major question to be addressed? If not, what information remains unknown?

4. Should the same approach strategy be employed with Michael and with Susan?

5. At this stage, how would you evaluate the CAC's prospects of securing a major gift from the Noseks?

Lincoln State University

After humble beginnings and a long fight to gain respect, as one civic leader put it, "Today everyone agrees, Lincoln State has arrived." Founded in 1915 as Lincoln Normal Teachers College, its mission was to "train tomorrow's teachers in up-to-date methods and techniques." This mission was relatively unchanged until after World War II, when the baby boom produced the need for more teachers and school administrators. The ratio of men to women students changed from 1:4 to 3:2.

More students brought about a need for a broader curriculum to satisfy changing legislative standards. The legislature altered the minimum teaching standards and abolished education as a major. A student who wanted to teach in the public schools was now required to select a major within the Letters and Sciences and to minor in education methodology. With this change came public recognition of Lincoln as a "full-fledged" university. In 1953 the name was officially changed to Lincoln State University.

Today, Lincoln State offers 36 majors in three colleges and serves 12,600 students. The 200-acre campus has retained its "small college feel" through periods of growth in the '50s and '60s. Lincoln's president, Dwight Standard, says, "The university is living proof that a human scale can be retained within a growing institution. All that is required is a lot of caring by everyone concerned."

Caring is a word one associates with Lincoln State. Its faculty place a high priority on teaching. Students choose Lincoln State over the more prestigious University of Lincoln because, as one student put it, "At U. of L. you are just a number. Here at Lincoln State, I am treated as an important person."

President Standard combines a strong record as an administrator with a reputation as a "people person." His interpersonal communication skills have earned him an excellent reputation with students and faculty alike. His ability to secure funding from the legislature is legendary. With his firm vision of Lincoln as a multi-disciplinary institution, he has provided budgets that the state government has funded at or near his request levels. But the recent economic recession has strained the state's resources, and reduced public funding is forecast for the present state budget. The immediate future looks bleak for Lincoln State.

President Standard is convinced that private support for Lincoln State is "an untapped resource waiting to be mined." Standard has recruited Richelle Lynn as vice president for institutional relations and provided a significant increase in resources to begin the process of reaching out to alumni, parents, and friends.

Prospective donor

Elsie Chapin has lived a quiet, conservative lifestyle for the past 85 years. As the only child of Fred and Ethel Chapin, successful Lincoln farmers, Elsie enrolled in Lincoln Normal in 1926, the first member of her family to attend college. The Depression made it difficult to find resources for tuition payments, but Elsie says, "I worked hard, skipped a few meals, and never forgot the faith my parents placed in me."

Elsie graduated in 1930 and found a job as a school teacher in the small lumbering town of Ferndale, Idaho. She remained a teacher for the next 45 years, but she never lost touch with Lincoln. She continues to refer to it as Lincoln Normal and feels it should return to its original mission of training teachers. Elsie moved into a retirement home near the university in order to attend cultural events, use the library, and take classes in the university's Leisure Learning Program. Rarely does a day go by that Elsie Chapin is not seen hurrying about the campus in pursuit of her many interests.

It was a chance encounter with President Standard in the library that put Elsie into the minds of the people in the development office. She informed the president that "Lincoln Normal is in my will, but I hope we both live a long time before you have to be concerned with all those legal matters." Standard laughed and replied, "Elsie, you'll outlive and out-learn us all."

Elsie admires Standard as an administrator but despairs at his "lack of compassion or understanding of what made Lincoln great." She attributes his failure to grasp the importance of teacher training to the fact that he graduated from the University of Lincoln in business communication. She recently told Richelle Lynn, "There are times I can't help but feel that I am the only one who remembers the foundation on which this university was built."

Elsie's best friends are Wilma Cormack, Lincoln State's librarian, and Phyllis Cheever, the director of the Leisure Learning Center. Both women are graduates of Lincoln State and have been associated with the college since the 1950s.

Elsie, who has never married, was devoted to her parents. They left their farm to live near her in the mid-1960s. Elsie's mother died in 1972; her father in 1975.

Development officer

Richelle Lynn likes to say that her career path was "more like a meandering that stopped to smell the flowers in every field along the way." But her humor belies her drive to succeed.

Richelle graduated with honors in teacher education from Lincoln State in 1972. She served as student body president in her senior year. Her interest in politics continued during a one-year internship in Washington, DC, at the

Department of Agriculture. She studied the role of agribusiness lobbies in the formulation of agricultural policy.

At the end of the internship she returned to Lincoln State to pursue a master's degree in education. During this time, she started a child-care center on campus. The university asked her to serve as interim director of student activities, and shortly afterwards, in 1975, she was named director. After 10 years in the director's role, she became vice president for student affairs.

When President Standard arrived in 1983, Richelle had recently resigned her position to return to her first love—teaching elementary school. She taught third grade for six years. When the position of vice president for institutional relations became vacant, Richelle's name was frequently mentioned for the post. Standard recalls, "Richelle had no direct background or experience in university relations, but she was a natural for the position." He persuaded her to leave teaching to return to Lincoln State.

In the three years since Richelle assumed her new role, annual giving has increased 65 percent and overall giving is up 72 percent. The private support goal for 1992 is $12 million. A capital campaign is in the feasibility study stage.

Richelle is considered a master at establishing rapport with Lincoln State's donors. She spends a considerable part of each week in the offices and homes of the university's supporters. At the top of her list is Elsie Chapin. They have developed a warm relationship with a high trust level on both sides. Elsie says, "Richelle understands the history of the university. As teachers we both realize the value of education in today's society."

Research background

Elsie Chapin's quiet, private demeanor has revealed little about her financial resources. Probate records indicate that her parents left her an estate valued at $750,000. Included in that valuation was a 640-acre farm valued at $350,000. Current sales of similar parcels indicate a value of $1,200 an acre.

In conversations with Richelle, Elsie has often referred to her financial adviser as "Robert," but no one knows anything about him—even his last name! Elsie is always up-to-date on the stock market and loves to discuss interest rate fluctuations. She regularly attends university lectures on the economy and the current investment climate.

Elsie's modest dress, small apartment, and 10-year-old car indicate that she spends little on herself. She has made numerous references to her "late Uncle Norman who left farming for banking." His picture is on Elsie's mantle beside photos of her parents. They apparently had a very close relationship.

Herbert Leighton, a local attorney, serves as Elsie's legal counsel. Leighton is on the Lincoln State Foundation. At foundation meetings, he excuses himself from any discussion of a possible gift from Elsie on the grounds of "attorney/client confidentiality." Leighton has served as Elsie's attorney for at least 30 years. He avoids any reference to Elsie's estate, except to acknowledge his role as legal counsel.

Gift records indicate a consistent pattern of giving since 1955. Elsie gives $1,000 a year to retain her membership in the President's Club. At her mother's death, she gave $5,000 to the university library to establish a special collections room. In 1977, Elsie gave $10,000 to the Leisure Learning Program to establish the Fred Elwin Chapin Memorial Lectureship. The Chapin Lectureship is focused on the history of rural life in northeast Lincoln, and the annual lecture is always a favorite of older citizens.

Unrecorded gifts to the university are numerous. Elsie has a habit of giving $100 checks to student-related causes. She always gives them directly to the person who requests the donation and consequently is frustrated when, at year's end, the university has no record of the gift. Richelle says, "It is an annual spring event that Elsie calls requesting verification of unrecorded gifts." Elsie always cites "an angry CPA who is a stickler for documentation."

Major gift focus

The research shows that Elsie has demonstrated several areas of interest in the university. She has supported the library over the years, but it is not clear whether this is due to a genuine interest or her close friendship with Librarian Wilma Cormack.

Elsie's soft spot for students is demonstrated by her continual gifts to their direct needs. She often sends financial aid to specific students, avoiding "official channels." She likes to refer to her "long list of student grandchildren." Richelle is aware of numerous letters from current and former students thanking Elsie for "her support and encouragement." These "grandchildren" stay in touch with Elsie long after they graduate.

Finally, Elsie's strong belief in continuing education is demonstrated by her active involvement in and financial support of the Leisure Learning Program. The program's emphasis on learning for retired persons is obviously very important to Elsie, as it was to her parents who were always taking short courses put on by the program.

Assignment

You are Richelle Lynn. You and President Standard are reviewing a letter from Elsie rejecting a visit from the consultant hired to do the capital campaign feasibility study. The letter is polite but firm. Elsie writes, "Richelle knows everything there is to know about me. My love for the university is unabated. I don't wish to waste your consultant's time with redundant information."

You and Standard agree that Elsie is key to the capital campaign. Her gift will "send an important signal to the older alumni who are on the fence." Now consider the questions below.

Prepare your answers in writing. Then, if possible, discuss your strategy with a colleague who has also read the case and prepared written answers. Together turn to Section 3 and read the discussion of Case C, beginning on page 151.

1. What is the next step? How should the university respond to Elsie's rejection letter?

2. If the university approaches Elsie for a gift to the campaign, what should the role of each of the following people be?

- President Standard?
- Richelle Lynn?
- Wilma Cormack?
- Phyllis Cheever?
- Herbert Leighton?
- Robert (the financial adviser)?

3. What is the focus of a major gift request? If no focus is obvious, what process should be used to develop one?

4. How would you orchestrate an approach to Elsie?

5. At this stage, how would you evaluate the chances of Lincoln State securing a leadership gift from Elsie in the forthcoming campaign?

St. Mark's Children's Hospital

St. Mark's Children's Hospital has been serving the people of central Kansas since 1934. The 280-bed hospital has enjoyed the respect of the community since its founding by the Sisters of the Sacred Heart. Despite great fluctuations in the economy, St. Mark's has grown steadily and modernized its plant on a regular basis.

St. Mark's enjoys an excellent relationship with the area's physicians. Although the original mission of the hospital was pediatric care, the board of directors has expanded the focus to include general family care.

The hospital director, Sister Mary Margaret, is affectionately known as "the iron fist in the velvet glove." She is tough minded, strong willed, and ready to fight for causes she feels are important to the hospital's future. Sister Mary joined the Sacred Heart Order in 1937. She served the hospital in several administrative roles before assuming the director's role in 1962. Under Sister Mary's guidance, the hospital plant has expanded over 75 percent; since 1975, bed count has doubled. A pediatric burn unit was added in 1987, and a cancer care unit is scheduled to begin construction within the next six months.

Administration is carried out by a 10-member board of directors. The board consists of three lay persons, three physicians, and three members of the Sacred Heart Order. Sister Mary Margaret serves as board president, a role she has held for the past 12 years. Sister Mary celebrates her 75th birthday in 60 days and has informed the board that she "intends to step aside and make way for younger blood." When pressed for a specific date, her reply is, "I am awaiting the Lord's guidance."

The board of directors has met informally and begun plans to honor Sister Mary. Several board members have suggested naming the new cancer care unit after her. No formal action has been taken because the board cannot legally be convened except by its president, Sister Mary.

Prospective donor

Henry M. "Buzz" Rice is the community's most successful real estate developer. His ability to make money in good and bad times is legendary. He builds just ahead of times of expansion and pulls back just in time for the inevitable economic downturn.

Everyone agrees that Buzz, a lifelong bachelor, is married to his work. Longtime friends comment on the joy Buzz gets from success and its financial rewards. He works hard; 15-hour days are the norm for Buzz. His staff is very loyal. According to his administrative assistant Sue Powell, "Under that gruff exterior is a warm-hearted teddy bear." That soft side isn't visible to any business associates, however. Buzz is known to negotiate over every point of a real estate acquisition until his wishes prevail.

Buzz recently entered the hospital for what he termed "a minor heart scare." Doctors were very close-mouthed about the nature of his illness. After three days of tests he was released with the warning, "Slow down, relax, and stop to smell the roses."

Buzz and Sister Mary are lifelong friends, or mortal enemies, depending on whom you ask. Buzz has served as a lay member of St. Mark's board of directors since 1945. According to other board members, Buzz opposes every idea put forth by Sister Mary. He argues vigorously in opposition until it becomes apparent that he is in the minority. Then, with a shrug, he votes with the majority "to preserve a unified front." Some board members, however, say that despite this, Buzz and Sister Mary have a mutual admiration society. He readily acknowledges her tough-mindedness and resultant successes. Sister Mary enjoys the inevitable clashes as a test of her ideas and leadership. She tells everyone that "Henry" (she refuses to call him "Buzz") has made major contributions in ideas and foresight over the years.

But Sister Mary has more than a contribution of ideas in mind for Buzz Rice.

Development officer

Bill Goode is "the strong, silent type." Although he is a person of few words, when he does speak, people listen.

Bill became executive director of the Sacred Heart Foundation in 1987. He has been in hospital fund raising since 1975. Bill combines a record of achievement in major gift fund raising with a quiet enthusiasm for the mission of the Sacred Heart Foundation. He says, "The children of this community have the highest quality medical care available in the Midwest."

Sister Mary and Bill work well together. She admires his organized approach to development work. He admires her willingness to "ask for the gift." The resultant gift totals are proof of their success. The recent campaign to expand the neonatal care unit was completed two months ahead of schedule. The original goal of $4.2 million was exceeded by $500,000.

Planning for the cancer care unit campaign is going well. The feasibility study suggests that the original goal of $15 million will be difficult without a lead gift of at least $3 million. Bill and Sister Mary agree that Buzz Rice is the person who must be asked to make the lead gift.

Research background

Calculating the assets of Buzz Rice is a much easier task than estimating his net worth. Public records reveal his direct ownership of real estate to be valued at $33.5 million. Corporations in which Buzz is the majority stockholder exceed $12.7 million.

Buzz is known for his conservative approach to investing. He likes to remain in total control of projects and is loath to take on excessive debt. For a man of wealth and position, he lives quite modestly.

Since almost all of Buzz Rice's holdings are private, it is difficult to estimate his net worth. The research staff has enough information to support "net assets in excess of $25 million." This estimate is far less than the commonly held figure of "$40-50 million." Buzz dismisses all discussion of his wealth with a reminder that "land and paper profits leave little cash in my pockets."

Since 1985 Buzz has made an annual gift of $100,000 to the hospital. Bill made a direct ask of $1 million for the neonatal care unit, but Buzz said that "now was a bad time." Three months later, he gave $350,000 to put the project over the goal. Buzz has no other philanthropic interests beyond St. Mark's Hospital. Gifts to other community needs have rarely exceeded $5,000.

Recently Buzz sold one of his largest holdings, a 132-acre commercial parcel, to ACTO Insurance Trust for a reported $13 million. Details of the transaction in public records indicate that Buzz received a $3 million down payment and holds a first mortgage of $10 million payable over 15 years.

At a recent board meeting, Buzz expressed rare agreement with Sister Mary that board members "needed to step forward boldly if St. Mark's is to move ahead." He pledged to give $200,000 to the annual fund.

Major gift focus

There seems to be unanimous agreement on gift focus. The cancer care unit is foremost in everyone's mind. The estimated construction cost of $15 million represents the largest project ever contemplated by St. Mark's. The consultants' gift table is also accepted by everyone. The $3 million lead gift was discussed by the hospital board of directors at three meetings before the campaign was officially adopted.

Buzz Rice remained silent during discussions about the campaign, except to express his support with a loud "yes" vote when the project was approved.

Assignment

You are Bill Goode. Sister Mary Margaret has asked you to prepare a strategy paper on approaching Buzz Rice for a leadership gift. You decide to include the Rice gift approach in a comprehensive campaign strategy report. Please answer the questions below.

Prepare your answers in writing. Then, if possible, discuss your strategy with a colleague who has also read the case and prepared written answers. Together turn to Section 3 and read the discussion of Case D, beginning on page 152.

1. Do you concur with the commonly held opinion that Buzz Rice is key to the success of the cancer care unit campaign? Why or why not?

2. Do you have sufficient research on which to gauge the ask level? If not, what additional data do you require?

3. What should your objectives be?

4. Who should be included in the ask meeting? Why?

5. How should the gift level be approached?

6. At this stage, how would you evaluate St. Mark's prospects for obtaining a gift of $3 million from Buzz Rice?

Case E

Kamps for Kids/
Nature Outreach

I t all started with a Johnny Carson show in 1969. Viewers saw three adults from New York City who had never been out of the city. One man lamented that he "had never been North of 155th." This preyed on the mind of one viewer, John Rodee, who tried to imagine a childhood without discovering the joys and mysteries of the rural countryside.

Talking with others, Rodee discovered a mutual interest in forming an organization to take children out of the inner city for a camping experience in upstate New York. A board of 15 friends was formed, and Kamps for Kids was born. In the early years the group rented existing summer camps on a weekly basis. As the program expanded, however, it became difficult to find suitable space. Moving equipment and continually uprooting staff became a growing problem.

Rodee was an enthusiastic fund raiser for Kamps for Kids. He put together a coalition of individuals, corporations, and foundations to underwrite the programmatic expenses. On a visit to the Thomas Supermarket headquarters, he met the founder and CEO Edgar Thomas. As Rodee talked about the program, it was obvious that Thomas "caught the vision." Rodee relates, "Ed Thomas asked me to rerun the little video we had put together. It was then I knew that he shared our concerns."

Thomas invited Rodee to his weekend retreat to share the Kamps program with his wife Ruth. As Rodee drove past the entrance sign to Thomas's Lakeview Farms, he knew he had found the permanent site for Kamps for Kids. After touring the 400-acre farm, Rodee told the story of inner-city kids who had never seen a cow, ridden a horse, or swum in a lake. Edgar and Ruth Thomas peppered Rodee with questions. At the end of the day, Edgar said, "Ruth and I enjoyed hearing about your program. We'll give it a lot of thought."

For three months, Rodee heard nothing. A phone call to the Thomases was not returned. Rodee's initial enthusiasm waned, and he all but forgot his visit to Lakeview Farms. One day a letter arrived from a Manhattan law firm announcing the "intention of Edgar and Ruth Thomas to gift 100 acres of Lakeview Farms to the Kamps for Kids program." Included in the gift was the right to use the 75-acre lake located on the undeeded land retained by the Thomases.

The land gift occurred in 1977. Over the years the program grew and became even more successful. If invited, Edgar and Ruth would walk over to the camp to join in the craft activities and watch the children tend the camp garden or attempt to milk a cow. Although they talked little, it was evident that the Thomases were pleased with their gift. Although invited, neither would join the board of directors. Edgar said he didn't want to "spend any more time doing what I do all day, sitting in meetings and passing on policy decisions."

Over the years, the focus of Kamps for Kids changed. Members of the board became more interested in environmental issues, especially ecology and conservation. Programmatic expenses were increasingly underwritten by conservation and environmental groups. Several corporation and foundation grants were obtained to carry out educational programs on environmental issues.

In 1983, the board of directors officially changed the name of the organization to Nature Outreach. The Kamps for Kids program became a part of a larger agenda. The board adopted a four-point mission statement which stated that priority concerns were to teach:
- concern for ecological matters;
- awareness of environmental issues;
- conservation of resources; and
- enjoyment of nature.

John Rodee expressed his regret at the loss of the original emphasis on camping, but told everyone, "I guess we have to change with the times."

Edgar and Ruth Thomas became even more remote, however, and they stopped making visits to the camp. Requests by board members for update meetings were turned down.

Prospective donors

Edgar Thomas, age 72, was born in Long Island. His parents could not afford a hospital stay, so he was delivered by a midwife in a bedroom above the family grocery store. By the time Edgar was 16, he knew as much about the grocery business as his father did. He dropped out of school to concentrate on expanding Thomas Groceries to additional locations in the growing Long Island suburbs. By 1945, he had five stores. In 1952, the name was changed to Thomas Supermarkets. The 93-store chain became known for its concern for service and low prices. When his father died, Edgar became president and CEO.

Ruth Cummins, age 68, was born and raised in New York City. Her father was a wealthy banker. According to a friend, "Ruthie combined charm, brains, and energy into an outgoing personality." She graduated cum laude from Columbia in theater arts. She began a career on the New York stage and soon was receiving larger and larger parts.

Ruth recalled, "It was either fate or chance that I met Edgar." She accompanied her father to a dinner for major customers of the bank and met the shy, bachelor supermarket baron. Until meeting Ruth, Edgar confessed, "All

I knew was work and more work. Ruth opened up a whole new world for me."

Their 40-year marriage produced four children. All are successful in their careers, but only their youngest daughter, Laurel, chose to go into the supermarket business. Edgar takes great pride in Laurel's business acumen and says, "She knows more about the business than her old man."

Development officer

Elaine Benner literally walked into her job. While out hiking with a group of friends, she stopped at the Nature Outreach camp to see the program and to buy some of the crafts for sale at the camp store. She was impressed with what she saw and excited about the kids' genuine concern for the environment.

Conservation of resources has always been a priority concern for Elaine. Her studies at Radcliffe centered on environmental science. She continued her studies at Oxford, obtaining a master's degree by reading in biology and ecosystems.

It was at Oxford that Elaine first met Laurel Thomas. They had similar interests and backgrounds. "Being Americans in a strange land brought us together" they told friends. Their friendship has remained strong in the 10 years since Oxford. Elaine pursued a career as assistant curator at the New York Museum of Natural History, and Laurel began to work for Thomas Supermarkets.

After she returned from her hiking trip, Elaine could not forget the excitement she had felt for the Nature Outreach program. She contacted the program's headquarters and offered to do some volunteer work. She became one of the most active volunteers the program had ever had, and eventually she was asked to co-chair the annual fund-raising appeal. Through Elaine's energy and innovative ideas, the goal was exceeded by 40 percent.

In November 1988 the board asked Elaine to join Nature Outreach as vice president for development. She has continued her earlier successes, and overall fund raising has increased, on average, 22 percent annually in the past four years.

Elaine did not learn about Laurel's connection with Nature Outreach until she had accepted the development job. When Laurel explained her parents' gift of the land for the camp, she added, "Dad doesn't like the way it has changed. He says he can't stand 'those damn tree huggers,' and that it's not really camping anymore." Since that conversation, Elaine has wondered how to win the Thomases back as supporters and donors.

Research background

A perusal of the research files on Edgar and Ruth Thomas is a lesson in how formal and informal research are integrated into a meaningful whole.

There is quite a bit of material on the Edgar Thomas success story. The growth of the grocery store into a tri-state supermarket chain has been chronicled by no fewer than 11 publications. The Thomas chain's ability to produce 21 years of increased net profits through widely varying economic times is considered a business miracle. Laurel Thomas has been credited with continuing the unabated growth through aggressive building and modernization programs.

Ruth Thomas's role as a leader in civic and philanthropic activities has also received considerable media attention. When Ruth chaired the mayor's Committee on Racial Equality, she receiving grudging admiration from people from all the different viewpoints. Her work in promoting repertory theater in low-income areas has been very successful in marshaling funds from New York's corporate sector.

Laurel has very limited time outside her new role as chief operating officer for Thomas Supermarkets. But she has devoted time and financial support to Operation Greenpeace. Recently Laurel agreed to chair the Conference on Environmental Concerns: Vision 2020. All indications are that Laurel is providing balanced leadership and keeping the conference agenda at a high level.

The bulk of the informal research on the Thomas family is in two groups. The first is a chronicle of contacts with the Thomases by John Rodee in the early and mid-1970s. John was meticulous in preparing debriefing memos following his many meetings. He captured the "feel" of meetings through direct quotes and careful analysis of "what wasn't being said but was being communicated." John was a good listener, and his research notes demonstrate his skill.

The second group of research revolves around Elaine Benner's considerable knowledge of the Thomas family. Both Ruth and Laurel Thomas consider Elaine a close friend of the family. Elaine has been very careful to separate her professional role at Nature Outreach from her friendship with the Thomas family. Everyone is aware, however, that Elaine would like to rekindle their interest in the program.

Laurel recently told Elaine that the family has set up a family foundation to help bring some order to their many charitable interests. Initial funding for the foundation was $2 million, but it appears that the short-term goal is to put $20 million in endowed funds. Laurel said, "All the details aren't finalized, but Dad is especially anxious to put his affairs in order. The foundation is a high priority to him and consumes all his free time."

Perhaps the most important piece of research came from a brief conversation Edgar had with Elaine at a recent family barbecue at the Lakeview Farms. Edgar looked across the lake and said, "I always thought we'd donate this property to Kamps for Kids to start an old-fashioned working farm, but they don't seem interested in that sort of thing anymore." Elaine asked, "Did you ever tell anyone about your interest?" Edgar smiled and said, "I was never asked."

Major gift focus

The Nature Outreach Board has recently voted on a new list of needs requiring private support. This list includes:
- establishing a demonstration tree farm;
- preparing an educational class on nutrition and the environment;
- building a center for housing current displays of relevant learning materials; and
- investigating the establishment of a responsible consumerism center.

Elaine supports each of the priorities and feels there is broad support among major donors for these needs. Her concern is that each priority will require approaching donors whose present focus is underwriting general programmatic expenses. The goal for program underwriting for the current year is $600,000.

Assignment

The major gift committee is meeting tomorrow. Reviewing the agenda, Committee Chair Dewey Eastberg remarks, "I don't see Old Man Thomas on our list of prospects anymore. Shouldn't we try to approach him sometime?" You are Elaine Benner, and it's your job to advise the committee. Now consider the questions below.

Prepare your answers in writing. Then, if possible, discuss your strategy with a colleague who has also read the case and prepared written answers. Together turn to Section 3 and read the discussion of Case E, beginning on page 153.

1. Is now the time to prepare an approach strategy toward the Thomas family? What factors should you consider in making this decision?

2. Who are the "players" in the Thomas family in considering a major gift? What is each person's role and influence?

3. You have a close friendship with the Thomases. What are the benefits and drawbacks of that friendship?

4. Given the past and present solicitation record, what is your primary objective with the Thomas family?

5. Who should take the lead from Nature Outreach in the Thomas cultivation?

6. What should the gift focus be?

7. How should the gift level be approached?

8. At this stage, how would you evaluate Nature Outreach's prospects of obtaining a major gift from the Thomas family?

Case F

Weston Symphony

At one time, Weston, Virginia, was another one of those indistinguishable suburbs of Washington, DC, which served as a bedroom community for thousands of commuters. But thanks to energy, location, and environment, its identity crisis was resolved in the mid-1970s.

Everyone agrees that Dr. David K. Ball, chair of the Department of Music at Weston University, was the catalyst behind the establishment of the Weston Symphony. With Ball's leadership and the support of a large group of enthusiastic volunteers, the symphony was founded in 1976. Drawing on the talents of professional musicians from eight colleges and universities in DC, Virginia, and Maryland, the symphony became an instant success, both economically and musically.

Critical reviews praised the Weston Symphony as "ranking with the finest established symphonies in its ability to present a wide range of highly polished, professional offerings." Dr. Ball, a distinguished conductor himself, led a national search to find a first-rate musical conductor. He was very fortunate to find Gunther Shushkin, assistant conductor with the Boston Symphony.

The Weston Symphony's business side was handled by Robert Mawditt, a veteran of 20 years of successful management of the Los Angeles Symphony and now retired to the DC area. According to Ball, Mawditt was "a genius at keeping the artists and auditors happy, the books balanced, and the hall filled with paying customers."

By 1985, the symphony had concluded a successful $15 million fund drive to build a symphony hall. The design and acoustics were hailed as being "in the same class as America's best classical music venues." With the completion of the symphony hall, season ticket subscriptions rose to 1,200, representing 80 percent of capacity. The upper-class Weston community embraced its symphony with renewed joy. It seemed that everyone was happy with the relationship. Everyone, that is, except E.B. Jackson.

Elizabeth Bacon Jackson, known since birth as E.B., has been variously described as "a wild-eyed, left-leaning activist" and "one of this nation's foremost medical authorities on nutrition." Both accurately capture the many facets of E.B. Jackson's past and present activities.

E.B. was born in 1940 to wealthy parents in Marin County, California. She graduated from UC Berkeley in 1962, summa cum laude in zoology. Her professors described her as "bright, witty, gifted, and formidable." E.B. chose to continue her pursuit of a medical degree at Johns Hopkins University. She completed a residency in endocrinology at Massachusetts General Hospital in 1968.

But the list of E.B.'s notable accomplishments captures only a small part of her interests and passions. While at Berkeley, she was a leading activist for equal rights. As E.B. says, "I spent more time on the steps of Sproul Hall screaming for social change than I did studying in the library." It seemed that E.B. was involved in all of the major events of that era: the Selma March, Woodstock, and the March on Washington, where Martin Luther King set forth the rights of "the poor who seek freedom and justice."

E.B. has continued to combine a career of professional achievement with social activism. She writes extensively about nutrition and obesity both for academic journals and for the general audience. According to a *New York Times* book reviewer, her best-selling books, *The Fat Feminist* and *Fat and Forty,* "are changing the nation's attitudes on dieting and social acceptability based on outward appearance."

In the past few years, E.B. has focused her interests on nutrition for young mothers, child care, and educational reforms in the Washington, DC, black community to "rescue poor children of color who show academic promise, but continue to be warehoused in an impersonal system."

Another side of E.B. Jackson is her passion for music. She was a donor to the Weston Symphony capital fund drive to build the symphony hall. Despite the many demands on her time, she proudly states, "I've missed only one symphony concert, and that was Eastern Airlines' fault."

Over the years, E.B. has become increasingly aware that, in her words, "The Weston Symphony audience is almost all white, all rich, and all like-thinking." She admits to overstatement, but feels her criticism comes close to capturing the reality of the situation. She has voiced her opinion to many members of the symphony's board of directors. To date, the only response has been a polite acknowledgment of the problem.

Development officer

If E.B. Jackson is distinguishable by her wide-ranging pursuits, then Robert S.K. Brown is notable for the seeming narrowness of his interests.

Bob was born into immense wealth. As the only child of a family who controlled a major natural resources conglomerate, he enjoyed the love of parents who lavished their attention—and their money—on him. He had toys and experiences most children only dream about.

Life changed for Bob when he attended an elite preparatory school on the East Coast. Boarding with 200 other boys was traumatic, but he quickly adjusted to the new life and became a well-liked leader in his class.

At Princeton, Bob was president of the Young Republicans Club and actively campaigned for Richard Nixon in his successful bid for the U.S. presidency. Bob's classmates recall that "Bob never questioned the agenda of the political right. He embraced their cause as his own and was one of the campus's most articulate advocates for conservative causes."

Bob also appreciates good music. Like E.B. Jackson, he has never missed the chance to attend a concert. When an opportunity arose to serve as an intern with the New York Symphony, he eagerly applied for the position. His enthusiasm and musical knowledge so impressed the selection panel that he was chosen for the internship by a unanimous vote.

It was Bob's intention to concentrate on the artistic side of the operation, but he was increasingly drawn to the side of private fund raising. For Bob, it was a natural combination of the duty his parents had instilled in him at an early age to give money back to the community and his own strongly held belief that people should support the activities they enjoy. Following graduation, Bob went to work for the Chicago Symphony as a development officer. He joined the Weston Symphony six months ago as director of development. When Bob began to review the files of existing donors to educate himself about the support base, E.B. Jackson's file fascinated him.

Research background

Research on E.B. Jackson is extensive and up-to-date. Previous development plans were to approach E.B. for a major gift, but they were abandoned when the director of development resigned. Bob Brown received a full file on an abandoned contact.

Each time E.B. had voiced her opinion about the lack of racial and economic diversity in the symphony audience, it had been called into the development office and noted in the file, but there was never any follow-up.

According to the file, E.B. held a part-time position at the Johns Hopkins Medical School. A member of the board who held a similar appointment estimated her annual salary at $70,000. As a practicing physician in a small group practice, E.B. saw patients three days a week. Estimated income was $100,000-150,000 a year. Academic journal articles were gratis, but her general audience books were best-sellers. Sales of her last three books totaled $750,000. Estimated income, assuming a 15 percent author's rebate, was $112,500. Speaking fees, at $5,000 per appearance, are estimated to be $100,000-125,000 per year. (E.B. donates her fees to the many causes she supports.)

Her townhouse has an estimated value of $500,000. A search of records reveals a one-third interest in a medical office building valued at $2 million (current building indebtedness is unknown). E.B.'s $5,000 contribution to the symphony hall fund was written on a check marked "Harold and Cora Jackson Trust, Boston." Efforts to discover details of the trust have been fruitless. Her annual contribution to the sympony is $1,200, and this contribution entitles her to attend six concerts in an area reserved for Sustaining Members.

Brown has never met E.B. and, after reviewing the file, he remarked, "We know so much about E.B.'s financial position, but so little about the person."

Major gift focus

At a recent retreat, the board decided that audience enhancement is a major concern. Although the present concert season is a sellout, attempts to expand the season were disappointing. Attendance at a special summer series had been projected at 1,000 per concert, but averaged fewer than 650.

The board agreed to meet again in 60 days to review Bob Brown's plan to boost attendance. Bob began by gathering the board's views and marketing ideas.

Assignment

You are Bob Brown. You decide to attempt to meet E.B. Jackson. Please answer the questions below.

Prepare your answers in writing. Then, if possible, discuss your strategy with a colleague who has also read the case and prepared written answers. Together turn to Section 3 and read the discussion of Case F, beginning on page 155.

1. What are your objectives in a meeting with E.B.?

2. How should E.B. be approached? By letter? Phone? Introduction through a third person?

3. What are the key discussion areas? What will this discussion accomplish?

4. What looms as possible communication barriers? How might you overcome these barriers?

5. Where should the meeting be held?

6. Who should be included in the meeting?

7. How should gift focus be approached?

8. How should the question of gift level be approached?

9. If the first meeting achieves the established objectives, what alternate follow-up questions do you suggest?

10. At this stage, how would you evaluate the Weston Symphony's potential to obtain a major gift (mid-five figures) from E.B. Jackson?

Jamesfield Academy

Jamesfield Academy, the first independent school west of the Mississippi River, was founded in 1902 by Elias P. James, a Harvard-educated mathematician, who had moved west in 1895 to serve as headmaster in Seattle, Washington. James's dream was to establish an independent secondary school with the same academic discipline he had received as a child in the East. As more and more people moved westward, the idea took hold. Starting with 14 first- through sixth-grade students, Jamesfield was founded, with Elias James as headmaster.

The origins of Jamesfield were modest. The school met in three rooms of the Kincaid Mansion on Queen Ann Hill. Each year brought two or three new students. In 1910, the school was moved to a vacated dairy farm north of Seattle. Elias James described the setting as "reminiscent of a John Constable landscape of the English countryside." The 55-acre farm had a large stone house with 14 rooms. Six outbuildings were situated around the farm. A large stream bisected the property.

In 1915, the academy expanded to secondary (grades 1-8) and postsecondary (grades 9-12) education. The student population had grown to 53. A boarding option was added, and 21 students occupied the two dorms in the upper floors of the main house. Elias James faithfully guided the academy for 28 years. By the time he retired in 1930, Jamesfield had added a gymnasium, two sports fields, a classroom building, and two dormitories to house 80 boys and girls.

Esther Johnson recalls, "I entered Jamesfield on September 1, 1914. Walking up to the main building with my mother and father seemed like a death march. Out of the doorway popped a Charles Dickens character, complete with sideburns, mismatched jacket and trousers, and a twinkle in his eye. This was my introduction to the legendary Elias P. James."

Today, Jamesfield is highly regarded for its academic rigor, its excellent physical education program, and its placement record with the Ivy League schools in the East. The 243 students are, for the most part, well above average in intelligence and very industrious. The ratio of boys to girls is 3:4. Boarding students have continued to increase, and today there are 156 students living on campus.

Donald Barbour became headmaster in 1978. He is urbane and shows the reserve of his British upbringing. The son of a wealthy wool merchant, Barbour was educated at Eton and Cambridge. He was hired as head from St. John's Academy, where he was dean of students. Barbour is shy and occasionally stammers in a small-group or one-on-one conversation. However, in front of a large group of students or parents, he comes alive. Charlotte Johnson Weber says, "No one can advance the case for independent schools better than Don Barbour. He renews my pride in Jamesfield every time I hear him."

What Charlotte doesn't know is how important *she* may be to the future of her alma mater.

Prospective donors

It is difficult to describe the Johnson family. Everyone remarks that it's hard to believe so many different individuals could come from the same family.

Esther Johnson, 84, Jamesfield class of 1926, is the matriarch of the Johnson clan. She is short, wily, and full of energy and strongly held views. She urges children to participate in sports because "a strong body and strong mind depend on each other." Each of her three children, William, Charlotte, and Jeremy, attended Jamesfield as boarding students even though their home was only five miles from the academy. Esther says, "The core of education is the boarding experience. The classroom is the formal education. The students' experience in interacting with others is the real education."

Elmer Johnson met Esther at Jamesfield in 1920. He always said it was love at first sight. Esther was intrigued by his constant questioning of the teachers, especially in the science classes: "Elmer never settled for simple answers. He demanded the whole story and then drew his own conclusions," she says.

After graduating from Jamesfield, Elmer started a pharmaceutical company, which grew rapidly. Prior to the antitrust laws, he also owned a large chain of pharmacies throughout the Northwest. Elmer died of a heart attack in 1972, and a few years later the businesses were sold for a reported $12 million.

Today William, 60, handles all the family's investments. Esther says, "William has the same shrewd business sense as his dad. He can spot a good investment ahead of everyone else."

Daughter Charlotte, 57, is her mother's best friend and constant companion. Both are active in a wide variety of civic and social organizations, but their first love is unquestionably Jamesfield Academy. Esther has been on the academy's board of governors since 1972. William and Charlotte have alternated on the board since 1976. William is a champion of the idea to expand the science curriculum. Charlotte wants to expand the liberal arts offerings, especially in the area of language and geography. "We are a global society," Charlotte explains. "Preparation for leadership in that society must include a knowledge of cultures, languages, and differing world views."

All of the Johnson family agree on one thing: Jamesfield must continue its strong emphasis on physical education.

Jeremy Elmer Johnson, 50, has always been called "J.J." He is shy and unassuming and rarely volunteers an opinion. He prefers the world of teaching economics. As a postsecondary teacher at Jamesfield, he claims he has the "world's best job, with good students and good subjects." When pushed, he admits that low pay and mediocre facilities are an obvious drawback.

J.J. has always received support from the family trust to supplement his modest salary. Esther is proud of J.J.'s personal contribution to Jamesfield.

Development officer

Lori North has to remind herself constantly that she is the director of development at Jamesfield. Ten years ago, she was the divorced mother of three, with little work experience and a formal education that ended with her junior year of high school.

A chance meeting with Charlotte at a YMCA job fair changed her life. She confessed her situation to Charlotte and laid out her dreams to attend college at night while playing the dual role of parent and breadwinner during the day. Charlotte helped Lori find a job at the bookstore of the local college so she could be closer to her classes. She also found a special scholarship for returning women. Lori has always suspected that the anonymous scholarship donor was Charlotte.

Upon graduation, Lori went to work in the college development office as director of phonathon operations. Two years later, she was promoted to director of annual giving.

In 1985, Donald Barbour told her about the newly created post of director of development at Jamesfield. The position was established by the Johnson Family Trust, which gave a three-year grant to underwrite the salary and program expenses. Lori had been recommended for the position by Charlotte.

Lori has established herself well within the school and with the board of governors. Her ability to establish rapport with a wide variety of donors is well-known by everyone at Jamesfield. Lori estimates that she meets with 20 donors a week. Her work has resulted in an annual fund increase averaging 23 percent over the past six years.

Included in her meeting schedule is a weekly visit with Esther Johnson. Esther lives by herself, and she is lonely in spite of her busy life. She looks forward to Lori's visits. She appreciates her enthusiasm for Jamesfield. Lori calls Esther her "personal history book." Most of the school's donor research has come from Esther's clear recollection of the Jamesfield support base. She has an amazing memory for facts and figures, especially the gift potential of other donors. Lori suspects that Esther's network of "informants" has been carefully cultivated over the years.

Lori doesn't know how to describe Esther's habit of giving her a $600 check "for the needs of the academy" at every visit. At times, she thinks it's a bribe to assure future visits, and at other times, she thinks it's Esther's way of giving their meetings purpose. Whatever the reason, the weekly gifts totaled $30,000 last year.

Esther also uses their meetings to send messages to Donald Barbour. She admires his achievements as head, but is bothered by his obvious discomfort in one-on-one conversations. Last week, Esther lamented that "Elmer's tragic death went unnoticed and unrecognized by Jamesfield." When Lori pointed out that the quad was named for Elmer, Esther didn't reply.

Research background

The research file on the Johnsons is embarrassingly small. Updating the file is always on Lori's "to do" list, but it never gets done. Lori knows she could write a book on the Johnson family, but agrees that a summary sheet is the place to start.

The Johnson Family Trust has assets of $21 million. Annual gifts to other organizations average $6,000, in addition to the $100,000 annual donation to Jamesfield Academy. The decisions are made by Esther and her three children. J.J. told Lori, "As far as the trust is concerned, we are all equal, but Mom reserves the right to cast five deciding votes when the need arises. Fortunately, we usually agree."

The trust grows annually, and distributions are usually at less than 10 percent of the value of the trust corpus. Their pattern of giving rarely varies and has become even more fixed in recent years.

Major gift focus

At the urging of Donald Barbour, the board of governors brought in an architectural firm to develop a long-range facilities plan. The consultant outlined the following major needs:

• The gymnasium is in need of major renovation at an estimated cost of $600,000.

• Classroom space is overcrowded and doesn't meet new requirements. Estimated cost for a new classroom building is $1.2 million and remodeling an existing space an additional $175,000.

• The dormitory buildings need major remodeling or replacement. Estimated cost for remodeling is $700,000; for a replacement facility, $1.4 million.

The consultant developed a plan showing 10 new buildings. After considerable debate, the board adopted the following priorities for additional facilities:

1. A multipurpose indoor sports facility. The building would hold physical education classrooms, offices, a basketball arena, and an indoor track. Estimated cost: $3.5 million.

2. A performing arts center to house a 700-seat hall, blackbox theater, and a large foyer to serve as a focal point for donor entertainment. Estimated cost: $2.1 million.

3. Replacement of the existing dormitory facility. The new facility would accommodate 50 additional boarding students. Estimated cost: $2 million.

The total facility needs list was set at $8,375,000.

William Johnson then made a motion to undertake a capital campaign feasibility study, but Esther spoke against the motion, and the board tabled it.

Assignment

You are Lori North. You receive a call from Esther Johnson. She says, "I know we're getting together tomorrow, but I wanted you to know that I've been thinking about you. I'm not getting any younger, and I need to think about what I should be doing for Jamesfield. Let's talk about that tomorrow. I'll be interested in your views." Now consider the questions below.

Prepare your answers in writing. Then, if possible, discuss your strategy with a colleague who has also read the case and prepared written answers. Together turn to Section 3 and read the discussion of Case G, beginning on page 157.

1. What is your objective for tomorrow's meeting? Has Esther already set the agenda?

2. What are the key areas of discussion?

3. What key research information is missing? How can it be obtained?

4. What is your recommendation on gift focus? How would you approach the subject?

5. How would you approach the question of gift level?

6. At this stage, how would you evaluate Jamesfield Academy's prospects for obtaining a gift in excess of $1 million dollars from the Johnsons?

Huntington University

Huntington University takes great pride in its alumni. And the generosity of the alumni for their alma mater indicates that the feeling is mutual. Last week, *Education Magazine* selected Huntington as the top-ranked university in the United States. Such honors seem to be a daily occurrence in the life of this prestigious institution. But such prestige has not always been accorded to Huntington.

In June 1873, Cyrus Pierpont Huntington held a press conference to announce the largest gift in the fledgling history of U.S. philanthropy. He established a $30 million educational endowment trust to establish Huntington College. The college charter envisioned "an institution devoted to the pursuit of knowledge in the sciences, arts, and professions." Under the skillful guidance of its founding president, Edward James Grey, the college established a broad-based undergraduate curriculum. Later, graduate colleges were begun in law, medicine, and theological studies. Huntington College officially became a university in 1957.

Today Huntington has 16,000 students, 107 major offerings, and degrees granted in three undergraduate colleges and five graduate schools. Its faculty is ranked among the top 10 universities in 11 different departments. Faculty honors include four Nobel Prizes (science and medicine), two Field Prizes (mathematics), and two Medal of Science winners (atmospheric science). The current president, Sarah Rhodes Bromfield, says, "Although it is difficult to rank institutions, Huntington University stands apart for its leadership in teaching, research, and service to the world community."

President Bromfield's statement wouldn't raise much of an argument with Huntington's internal or external constituencies. "Leadership for the Twenty-First Century" is the theme for the current $600 million comprehensive campaign. Only 16 months into the three-year campaign, the university announced a gift total of $475 million.

But the positive attitudes do not include Tom and Susan Boland, class of 1962.

Prospective donors

Susan Hansen was featured in the September 16, 1961, issue of the *Saturday Evening Post* as one of "Ten Young Americans on the Move." Her 4.0 GPA and Phi Beta Kappa membership were duly noted. A picture of Susan preparing for the 1962 Olympics showed her winning the NCAA Championship in the women's 400-meter relay. Despite her prowess in athletics, Susan declared that her ambition was to attend the London School of Economics to study marketing, a dream she fulfilled in 1964.

She then began her career as a marketing consultant with McFarland Consulting. After five years of advising others about business strategies, Susan says she "decided to see if my ideas applied to me." The founding of Hansen, Boland and Stein in 1970 enabled her to do this. Today current billings for the company exceed $15 million, and it is regarded as the international leader in marketing and product evaluation.

Thomas Hays Boland was an indifferent student, a dedicated practical joker, and Huntington's all-time leading scorer in basketball. His 43-point record in the 1962 NCAA basketball finals still stands. He always reminds Susan that, although he may have been two points behind her in GPA, they received identical diplomas.

While Susan was in London, Tom joined the sales staff of Baxter Brewing to "sell beer, talk sports, and push into new markets." After four years, Tom grew tired of sales and applied to Harvard Business School. The admissions committee gave great weight to the recommendations of two Huntington faculty who predicted a promising career for Tom. He fulfilled the promise and at graduation was ranked third in the class. Tom joined McFarland Consulting in 1967.

It is difficult to say who was more surprised to see the other. Susan says, "I hardly recognized the tall figure in the Brooks Brothers suit." Tom simply says, "I was a late bloomer. Besides, I was desperate to see Susan again." Adjoining offices and late-night projects served as the basis for romance. Tom and Susan were married, resigned from McFarland, and founded their own company in the same week. Tom remarks, "And on the seventh day, we rested."

Hansen, Boland and Stein profited under their joint guidance, but Tom grew restless. He wanted to run his own company. His opportunity came in 1989 when he was called into consultation with the Cumberland Flag Company. The owner was anxious to retire, and Tom offered to purchase the company. Susan was thrilled that Tom was getting the chance to realize his dream of taking on a failing manufacturing company and working to revitalize it. The first three years were devoted to reestablishing the company in its original markets to become the regional leader in sales of the American flag and other patriotic symbols.

The events of the Gulf War, while providing a boom in sales for the flag factory, convinced Tom and Susan of the great need for global conflict resolution; peace studies became a consuming passion.

Development officer

Jim Richards never left Huntington University. Following graduation in 1962, he went to work in the alumni office as director of the Alumni College. This job put him in contact with many of Huntington's older alumni. Jim's engaging smile, quiet determination, and unquestioned loyalty to Huntington made him a favorite of alumni, both young and old.

In 1971, Jim moved to the development office to become assistant director of major gifts. His friendships among the alumni proved a special asset. Jim led the staff in securing major gifts (over $25,000) in Huntington's first capital campaign. In 1980, Jim was appointed special gifts officer, with responsibility for gifts over $250,000.

Jim has had a "comfortable" relationship with Tom and Susan since their early years as undergraduates. Jim has quietly worked behind the scenes to arrange for the Bolands to serve on key university committees, speak to classes in the School of Management, and attend dinners with visiting VIPs. He has long urged the university's board of trustees to consider either Tom or Susan for membership. He laments, "They cancel each other out in the nomination committee. Half of the committee want Susan, and the other half vote for Tom."

Jim's interest in seeing that Tom and Susan "move in the highest circles" is bolstered by the knowledge that they have considerable wealth, both inherited and earned in their own right. The rumor that Hansen, Boland and Stein is to be purchased by a division of Chase Manhattan for $16.5 million has added to his concern.

Research background

Susan Hansen Boland's socially prominent family has been in the Blue Book since 1921. Her parents were both successful physicians in Cleveland, Ohio. The Hansen Clinic is regarded as the nation's leading diagnostic center. Susan's father died in 1987. Her mother, now 94, retired to their Palm Springs, California, home four years ago.

Susan is the beneficiary of a trust that provides $200,000 annual income. At her mother's death, an additional trust will double the income. The trust principal will be distributed in the year 2000, when Susan turns 60.

Hansen, Boland and Stein's sale price rumors are the only indication of possible company worth. Her two-thirds ownership for tax reasons (Tom sold his interest to her, for tax reasons, in 1984) indicates her share to be in the $10 million-plus category. Net value of the company is unknown.

Thomas Hays Boland comes from a "Mayflower" family. The Hays Brothers Bank is one of Boston's largest commercial banking houses. Both parents are alive and well in their mid-eighties. They divide their time between homes in Boston, the Florida Keys, and Nice, France.

Tom and Susan live well and entertain lavishly. Huntington President Sarah Bromfield is a frequent guest. She said in a note to the file, "No one can match Susan's flair for hosting a party or Tom's ability to tell a witty story." At a recent small dinner party, Tom and Susan shared their interest in global conflict resolution. In another debriefing memo, President Bromfield said, "There is no question that Susan and Tom care deeply about world peace. This isn't a fad with them. Both appear to be well read on the subject and eager to learn more."

The appraised value of Tom and Susan's home is $1.3 million. Their home in Palm Springs is valued at $600,000. Other California investment property is valued at $3.5 million. No data indicate the mortgaged amounts, but Tom always tells people, "We practice leveraging whenever possible."

A recent press clipping shows Susan holding a trophy beside her 1922 Rolls Royce. The paper noted its value at "over $1 million."

Tom and Susan have donated $1,500 annually for membership in the President's Club, $1,000 annually to belong to the Old Blue (the sports booster club), and $1,000 annually to sponsor a student peace vigil. The latter gift was initiated in 1990. Requests for larger gifts have been discouraged by the Bolands, since they claim to be "in the asset accumulation stage of our life rather than asset distribution." No formal proposals have ever been put in front of either Susan or Tom.

Major gift focus

Susan called President Bromfield with an unusual request. She asked that she and Tom be allowed to make a brief presentation to the university's board of trustees. When pressed for a subject area, Susan said, "Peace and conflict resolution, of course." The board allowed 15 minutes on the agenda.

The trustees braced themselves for a lecture on the university's lack of response to student requests to establish a program on conflict resolution. No one was more shocked than Sarah Bromfield when Tom and Susan stood before the microphone to announce their intention to "give a gift of $500,000, over five years, to immediately establish a chair in peace studies." The Bolands expressed the hope that Huntington University would take a leadership role in preparing for the day "peace breaks out all over the world."

There was applause around the table, but as soon as Tom and Susan left the room, the board chair called an unscheduled executive session. As Jim Richards got up to leave with other senior staff, the board chair said, "Jim, I'd like you to stay." A surprised Jim Richards sat down. The board chair began the executive session by remarking, "I don't know whether to laugh or to cry. Here, we've just heard an announcement of a half-million dollar gift, and I'm depressed." The discussion went on for 45 minutes. Finally, a motion was offered to "graciously thank Tom and Susan Boland for their generous offer of a chair but, regretfully, decline their offer for reasons of institutional economics." This motion was defeated 15-14. President Bromfield asked the board to table any action for two weeks to give her time to "advise the board on this matter." The board quickly adjourned the executive session and returned to an open meeting.

Assignment

You are Jim Richards. The day after the board meeting, President Bromfield called you into her office and said, "Jim we've got a big problem. The board will turn down the gift unless I come up with a solution to our problem." She outlined four concerns:

1. The university is facing a 2 percent cutback in budget in order to keep tuition increases in line with inflation.

2. At this time the university cannot begin a new program. Besides the financial costs involved, there would be no support from the academic staff to start a new program when existing areas are being cut back.

3. A chair requires a minimum gift of $1.2 million, and recruiting cannot begin until the entire sum has been invested for one year.

4. A chair cannot stand alone. The supporting programmatic costs would exceed $200,000.

President Bromfield concluded by saying, "Tom and Susan are wonderful people. Their cause is a priority for all of us. They will be one of our largest donors in the future if we handle this right." She paused a moment and said, "Jim, I need your help. What should I do?" She asked you to return two days later to discuss this issue. How should you advise President Bromfield? Please review the questions below.

Prepare your answers in writing. Then, if possible, discuss your strategy with a colleague who has also read the case and prepared written answers. Together turn to Section 3 and read the discussion of Case H, beginning on page 158.

1. From an external relations viewpoint, what is the problem?
2. What are your objectives in meeting with President Bromfield?
3. What would you advise President Bromfield? To accept or reject the gift?
4. Should a meeting be set with Tom and Susan Boland?
5. What would your objectives be at the meeting?
6. Who should attend the meeting?
7. Where should the meeting be held?
8. Is gift focus a problem? If it is a problem, how should it be solved?
9. How should the problem of gift level be approached?
10. At this stage, how would you evaluate Huntington College's prospects for resolving the problem and obtaining a gift in excess of $500,000 from the Bolands?

The Center for Gender Studies

I f ever an organization was born out of a perceived need, it is the Center for Gender Studies (TCGS). In 1970, the Ford Foundation received 34 requests for funding to support the study of women's issues. Other major philanthropic foundations reported a similar number of requests focused on women's concerns. Several foundations issued a joint request for proposals to establish a center to study gender issues. The response was overwhelming. The Hudson Foundation received and evaluated 126 proposals and finally awarded a five-year, $1 million grant to a group of well-known academicians who proposed, as a major focus, high-level research on the history of gender discrimination. The Center for Gender Studies began operation in February 1972.

The center attracted scholars from throughout the United States to study at its headquarters. Located next to Harriman University, TCGS had both the resources of a major university and the freedom to establish its independence. The center flourished for the next 15 years. During the Reagan Administration, however, government funding decreased and private foundations began to fund fewer and fewer of the center's proposals.

In 1987 TCGS hired its first full-time director of development. Despite her limited fund-raising experience, Phyllis Kaufman was the unanimous choice of the board of governors. Her persuasive writing skills far outweighed her lack of experience in donor cultivation and solicitation.

The center has an administrative staff of 11, including three academic research assistants. At any one time, the center has 15 scholars-in-residence. Each scholar is asked to make a public presentation of his or her work at one of the Thursday evening symposiums. It was at one of these events that Phyllis met the famous Ann Silverman.

Prospective donor

Some years ago Ann Silverman told the *New York Times* that she "grew up in a man's world, apprenticed in a man's trade, and succeeded on a woman's instincts." Always the battler, Ann opened doors for women in the fashion and fabrics industry.

Ann was born in Germany, but her parents immigrated to the United States well before World War II. Ann grew up in New York City in the 1930s at the height of the Depression. The family survived on her father's meager wages as a fabric cutter and her mother's piecework earnings in one of the city's notorious sweatshops.

In school Ann was an average student except in writing and art where she excelled. Her high school counselor, Mrs. Cluchi, urged Ann to go on to college to study fashion design. Over strong objections from her father, Ann entered Columbia University in 1941.

Ann first became attracted to politics when she managed the successful campaign of her friend, Barbara Marrs, the first women student body president. Ann says, "I quickly found out that if you were willing to shun the spotlight, you could achieve more power by directing the play itself." She worked in local elections for Democratic party politicians who promised social change, and she refused to become disillusioned when campaign rhetoric almost inevitably became empty promises after the candidate got into office. In typical Ann Silverman style, she threw her energies into attempting to ensure that candidates who supported women's rights continued to support them once they were elected.

While still at college, Ann became well-known in New York political circles for producing well-crafted position papers on equal rights and equal employment opportunities.

Upon graduation, Ann went to work as a design assistant for a fashion designer. She quickly discovered that she could design clothes for the "low-fashion" trade. She advanced rapidly. By 1950, she was the chief designer of clothes sold by Sears, Roebuck & Company and J.C. Penney's.

In 1952, Ann left to establish Anne Z Fashions. No bank was willing to underwrite this "risky venture." When pressed, bank officials admitted that her gender played a major role in their decision. Ann sold her car and mortgaged her townhouse to raise the $50,000 required to underwrite her first year of designing and manufacturing "sportswear" (a term often attributed to Ann).

By 1972, Ann's twentieth year in business, Anne Z Fashions was grossing $22.5 million in sales. Anne Z was one of the first American companies to utilize Pacific Rim countries to mass-produce clothes. Ann hired promising women designers and administrators to lead the growing company.

Business did not occupy all of Ann's time. She continued her early interest in politics. In 1980, she headed the New York delegation to the Democratic Convention. Her insistence on a strong women's rights plank won the admiration of many of the party leaders. She wrote speeches on social issues for numerous East Coast candidates.

Ann received "mixed reviews" on her successful suit to force an all-male club to admit her to membership. She said her motivation was "to allow women equal access to the seats of power, both in the board room and in the lunchroom."

In 1988, a TCGS scholar from Duke interviewed Ann as part of a study on the role of women in U.S. industry in the 1960s. Ann attended this scholar's lecture because she was "curious to discover how many people agreed with me on the lack of representation of women in the postwar industrial expansion."

Phyllis Kaufman greeted Ann at the door, gave her a nametag, and showed her to a reserved seat. Phyllis remembers this first meeting well because she was embarrassed that Ann's name was misspelled ("Anne") on the nametag, but Ann had laughed and said, "It happens all the time. That's what I get for starting a company named Anne Z Fashions. It sounded fancier at the time, but now everyone thinks my name is 'Anne.'"

Development officer

Phyllis Kaufman, 39, admits she would "rather write than talk, read than visit, and listen than propose." But beneath the shyness is a person who cares passionately about issues of social justice, especially gender discrimination.

Phyllis grew up as an only child in a home filled with love, interest in the arts, and lively discussion of the social issues of the day. Her childhood was spent listening to her parents and their friends debate issues of U.S. domestic and foreign policy. At an early age, she got in the habit of writing down the titles of books mentioned in these conversations and then reading them.

She excelled in college and graduated magna cum laude from Brandeis University. Although her best friend delivered the commencement address, it was Phyllis who wrote it. After graduation, she went to work for the American Red Cross as a grant-writer. She could compose a case statement and related appeal that would engage the most apathetic reader. The organization regretted losing her talents, but understood her strong interest in the offer from TCGS.

Gradually, Phyllis discovered that her shyness wasn't a liability when she met with prospective donors. She listened well, followed up quickly, and endeared herself to people with her quiet passion for the TCGS mission. Gift income rose 21 percent in her first year. By the end of her first five years, gift income was up 184 percent. In 1991, total gift income was $6 million. Despite these dramatic increases, the organization concluded that relying on annual fund drives was no longer sufficient. A capital campaign was necessary to bring in the level of support required to keep TCGS at the forefront of serious study of gender issues.

Phyllis hired an outside campaign counsel to conduct a feasibility study. After interviewing 70 people, the consultant concluded that a campaign goal of $30 million was reasonable—*if* TCGS "aggressively pursued a program of elevating existing supporters to major gift status." The gift table indicated the need for a lead gift of $5 million, two gifts of $2 million, and five gifts of $1 million. Phyllis knew that one of those lead gifts must come from Ann Silverman.

Research background

Ann Silverman is a favorite of both the society and the business press. She loathes the former and accepts the latter. The society press covers her leadership in Democratic party fund raising. She has personally raised over $50 million in campaign funds in the past 10 years. She is reputed to be one of the largest donors to the party.

Ann donated a lead gift, $2.5 million, in a Bonds for Israel campaign in 1989. She chaired the major gifts committee. Although the nickname "Arm-Twister Annie" doesn't please her, she admits that the results of her efforts do bring "a great deal of satisfaction."

The Anne Z Fashions company is privately held. Ann owns 64 percent of the stock, and the balance is held by employees and a few private investors. In 1987, a takeover was rumored, and the press estimated the sale price of the company at $230 million. The net value of Ann's holdings in the company was estimated at $150 million. In an interview with the *Wall Street Journal,* she commented on that figure. She said, "My creditors and the IRS will be pleased with the media's estimates of my net worth. My CPA firm is surprised, I am flattered, and my parents are proud. If only you were right."

Ann lives well. The condominium in Manhattan is valued at $3.5 million. No other real estate is held in her name in New York, but she has a country house in Vermont, including 50 acres of pasture land and valued at $1.2 million.

Phyllis visits with Ann on a regular basis. They are opposites. Phyllis is quiet and reserved, while Ann is outgoing, verbose, and a battler. She dominates the conversation. Phyllis enjoys hearing Ann's opinions and always lets Ann know what research programs TCGS has underway that address Ann's areas of interest. They find common ground and mutual respect in a love of writing: The power of the written word is one subject that invariably surfaces in their conversations.

Phyllis has written extensive debriefing memos to the file on her visits with Ann. She notes that Ann's collection of Impressionist art was appraised at $17 million. A Giverny "Water Lilies" painting by Monet is Ann's pride and joy. Ann's comment was, "It was worth every penny to have Monet as a permanent house guest." Phyllis hasn't been able to discover the value of the painting.

Ann gave her first gift to TCGS in 1987. In response to a year-end appeal, she sent a check for $5,000. The following year, she donated Anne Z Fashions stock valued at $7,800. Her annual gifts have increased each year. In 1991, she gave $16,200 in Anne Z stock. She has never been asked for a gift beyond her annual pledge.

Major gift focus

The reputation of TCGS depends on its ability to attract the nation's leading scholars. As new research topics come to the forefront, the center needs to be able to respond and sponsor research posts in those areas.

A citizen's advisory board, the Blue Ribbon Panel, was established to suggest priority areas for improvement in TCGS's program. The panel consisted of the mayor of New York City, the U.S. senator from New York, the head of the Garment Workers Union, and five academic staff who have been scholars-in-residence at the center in previous years. Ann declined an invitation to serve on this board. She explained to Phyllis, "The lay members are all dear friends, but I am over-extended for the next six months. However, I will be very interested in the panel's conclusions and recommendations."

Phyllis promised to give Ann a copy of the report as soon as it was issued.

The panel recommended four priorities for study:

- historical studies regarding the role of women in the armed services;
- women and political power;
- gender barriers in U.S. industry; and
- the gender challenges of increasing trade with Pacific Rim and Eastern Bloc countries.

In addition, the panel recommended that two wings be added to the TCGS headquarters to accommodate the increased office space needs.

The TCGS board of governors adopted the panel's conclusions and asked Phyllis Kaufman to develop a capital campaign plan.

Assignment

You are Phyllis Kaufman. As you were reviewing the campaign consultant's report, you discovered an important point you had overlooked in earlier readings: "Volunteer leadership is one of the keys to success in reaching established fund-raising goals." Now, as you prepare to call on Ann Silverman to deliver the Blue Ribbon Panel's report, consider the questions below.

Prepare your answers in writing. Then, if possible, discuss your strategy with a colleague who has also read the case and prepared written answers. Together turn to Section 3 and read the discussion of Case I, beginning on page 160.

1. What are your objectives in visiting with Ann?
2. What long-term objectives do you feel are important in future meetings with Ann?
3. What is the overall quality of the research you have assembled on Ann?
4. Where should the meeting be held?
5. Who should be included in the meeting?
6. How should you approach the question of gift focus?
7. How should you approach the question of gift level?
8. At this stage, how would you evaluate the likelihood of TCGS persuading Ann to chair the campaign?
9. At this stage, how would you evaluate the potential of TCGS to obtain a gift in excess of $2.5 million from Ann?

Case J

University Hospital

State University reflects 110 years of careful attention to its mission of teaching, research, and public service. It has earned its reputation as one of the nation's premier research educational institutions. Adding to that reputation is its medical school and health care facility, University Hospital.

University Hospital is widely regarded as the finest medical research center in the Southwest. Over its 73-year history, the hospital has been able to balance its obligation to medical research with a demonstrated concern for patient care. In recent years, the hospital has made major advances in the field of neurology. Specialization in neurological studies of the body's chemical effect on brain function has drawn world-famous researchers to University Hospital.

David Huetter, dean of medicine, and Donna Lee, director of the hospital, work well together, and their partnership is credited with creating a strong administration and a positive working environment. Chief of Psychiatry Randall Muncie says, "Donna and Dave are a true team. Any success we've enjoyed in our department is due to their concern for our welfare." It should be noted that the Department of Psychiatry recently received approval to add a 50,000 square-foot wing to the hospital to create additional lab, office, classroom, and patient-care facilities.

According to Dean Huetter, the hospital is "in a positive cycle of goodwill, finances, and facilities." Director Lee concurs, but forecasts major problems because of the federal government's unwillingness to cover a larger share of indigent medical care.

Community relations between the hospital and neighboring cities are excellent. This is largely due to a program that offers free clinical discussion groups on current medical concerns. Programs have centered on headaches, back pain, and heart attack prevention. At a recent program on mental illness, the audience was startled to hear Dr. Muncie declare that "Schizophrenia is the most damaging and widespread cause of mental illness among young people today."

In the audience were Martin and Karen Walters, who fought back tears as Dr. Muncie spoke.

Prospective donors

Martin and Karen Walters are both 55 and appear, at first meeting, to be a happy couple. As the parents of four children, they rejoiced a few years ago when their youngest child left home to attend college. But now their appearances mask a deep sorrow.

In 1986, Martin and Karen received a call from their 18-year-old daughter's roommate. She said, "Debbie is acting strange. She seems depressed and hardly talks." The roommate continued, "I just chalked it up to stress, but lately she has begun to talk to people who don't exist. I'm worried about her." The parents were alarmed and drove to the college to visit Debbie the next day. They were shocked at what they saw. Debbie was thin and pale and seemed to be agitated and anxious. Her parents persuaded her to go home with them to see their family physician.

The family doctor suspected drug use, but Debbie insisted that she had not used drugs of any sort, and her parents believed her. The doctor referred her to Randall Muncie at University Hospital. Debbie began a series of tests the following week. Martin and Karen will never forget the moment when Dr. Muncie told them the results—Debbie was suffering from schizophrenia. They also won't forget Muncie's compassion as he explained Debbie's illness to them.

Development officer

Karl Spicer is a problem-solver beyond compare. After graduating from college, he spent 14 years as a community liaison officer with the state Urban Renewal Agency. Karl seemed to like everyone, and everyone seemed to like Karl. The bigger the problem, the more the gusto Karl exhibited in finding a solution satisfactory to the parties involved.

But the years took their toll. Karl says, "By the age of 38, I was burned out. I was ready for a job that would show tangible signs of success. That's what attracted me to fund raising." Karl was hired as director of development and community affairs for University Hospital in 1981. More and more, he has concentrated on securing private funding for the hospital's seemingly insatiable needs.

Karl met Martin and Karen Walters through Randall Muncie. They had formed a support group for parents of children with schizophrenia. Karl's office helped with mailing a monthly newsletter, providing meeting space, and assisting in fund raising. In the past four years, Karen raised $350,000 from corporations and foundations to aid in the diagnosis of schizophrenia. Karl says, "Karen is the best volunteer fund raiser I've ever known. She has a story to tell and she tells it with strength, knowledge, and conviction." For her part, Karen considers Karl a friend and confidant.

Research background

As the *Texas Times* tells it, Martin Walters "discovered Ronald McDonald before anyone else in Texas." Martin secured contracts to build and operate

McDonald's fast food outlets in 32 cities in Texas. He now owns 103 restaurants. Through his skillful management, the Walters Group has expanded faster than its competitors and avoided a major debt load. Says Martin, "We don't break ground for a new restaurant unless we're making a profit on the last one."

Karl says his only estimate of the Walters' net worth came from a statement made by Martin that "a $50 million bank account doesn't buy an exemption from pain."

Karen taught school in the early years of her marriage but quit after their second child was born. Then she managed the books for the Walters Group until it became a full-time job. When her children were growing up, she divided her time between them and volunteer leadership in the University Community Church.

A real estate search shows properties held by Martin and Karen to be valued at $1.4 million. Additional properties held by the Walters Group are assessed at $73 million. Karl considers the assessed value to be very low.

Martin and Karen live conservatively. They built their present residence 17 years ago. They added a small stable, as Martin put it, to "get the girls through their horse years." Karen retorts, "Martin never got through *his* horse years, and riding remains his only hobby." The house, pool, stables, and three-acre lot are valued at $570,000.

Randall Muncie wrote in a recent debriefing memo that "Martin never hears Karen's pleas to slow down. When Debbie was finally institutionalized, Martin began working harder than ever. Now, 18-hour days are the norm." He goes on to say, "Karen has thrown herself into raising money. Martin has thrown himself into making money. Both deal with the pain differently. It's a miracle that they find any time to spend together."

Although the Walters have not been involved with University Hospital very long, their gift record is excellent. In 1986, the year Debbie's schizophrenia was diagnosed, her parents gave $50,000 to Dr. Muncie's study of the role of hormones in schizophrenia. The gift has increased annually to its present level of $160,000. Total gifts for this research project equalled $410,000. The Walters also give $20,0000 a year to underwrite the majority of the funding for the parents' support group.

Karen Walters' mother died last year. With part of the proceeds of the estate, Karen established a memorial fellowship in Dr. Muncie's lab. The endowment gift was $150,000.

In addition to their support of University Hospital, Martin Walters has focused his energies on the building of the Ronald McDonald House adjacent to the hospital grounds. According to a press release at the time of the ground-breaking, Martin donated $280,000 in a dollar-for-dollar match of donations given through his restaurant outlets. The hospice center has named the apartment wing in honor of Martin for "his unselfish devotion to the cause of helping young cancer patients and their families remain together during times of crisis."

Major gift focus

Recently Dean Huetter and Director Lee held a gathering of donors and prospects to discuss the long-range plans of the hospital. The group was separated into focus groups. In one group, Karen was a strong advocate of putting money into the research and diagnosis of schizophrenia. In another group, Martin was urging further expansion of the hospital to treat more patients.

When the results of the groups' deliberations were discussed, the Walters' differing points of view regarding future direction became evident. Martin advocated "bricks and mortar," while Karen wanted more basic research.

After the public-input sessions, the hospital board of visitors approved a long-range plan calling for spending $122 million over 10 years. Included in the 71-project plan were expanded research facilities and postdoctoral fellowships in basic neurology research.

Assignment

You are Karl Spicer. You have met with Dean David Huetter, Director Donna Lee, and Chief of Psychiatry Randall Muncie. It was agreed that you should "move forward to approach the Walters for a major gift toward the approved long-range projects." Muncie favors fellowships. Lee and Huetter favor money to add laboratory space for the Center for Studies of the Brain. At the next meeting, two weeks from now, you are to present a strategy for approaching the Walters. Now consider the questions below.

Prepare your answers in writing. Then, if possible, discuss your strategy with a colleague who has also read the case and prepared written answers. Together turn to Section 3 and read the discussion of Case J, beginning on page 162.

1. What major objectives would you suggest?

2. What key areas must you discuss with Martin and Karen Walters to better focus a proposal?

3. What information do you need to obtain that isn't revealed in existing research?

4. Where should the meeting be held?

5. Who should be included?

6. How should you approach the question of gift focus?

7. How should you approach the question of gift level?

8. At this stage, how would you evaluate University Hospital's prospects for obtaining a gift of more than $1 million dollars from the Walters?

Case K

Riverdale Art Gallery

I n 1945, America was alive with postwar planning and possibilities. The town of Riverdale, West Virginia, however, seemed to be just the same as it had been for the past 100 years. Coal was being mined, and young people were looking forward to two alternatives: Work in the mines for the rest of their lives or leave Riverdale to find work in the cities along the Eastern Seaboard. The majority left home to seek greater opportunities elsewhere.

No one was more aware of the decline of Riverdale than Elias P. Bronte, owner of Great Virginia Mining. Bronte knew business, and he knew the community was threatened if the trend was not reversed. He threw his considerable weight and wealth behind a community revitalization plan. Under his guidance, building began for a library, a movie theater, and a community sports center.

A booming economy and the resulting high demand for domestic coal stabilized the community. General Motors located a major plant in Riverdale. Other industrial plants followed the GM lead. By 1955, Riverdale was growing and prospering.

Elias Bronte loved art. He bought 18th and 19th century American paintings, and his collection of French Impressionists rivaled the finest collections in Boston and New York. He pondered the question of what to do with his collection after his death. The Muse d'Orsay in Paris, Great Britain's National Gallery in London, and the National Gallery of Art in Washington, DC, were all courting Mr. Bronte to acquire the collection. It was his daughter Mary who suggested the idea of building an art gallery in Riverdale "to plant the seeds of culture in the community which has been the lifeblood of Great Virginia Mining."

Elias liked Mary's idea. He established the Riverdale Art Gallery in 1958. His gift of $650,000 provided for completion of the construction of a 235,000 square-foot concrete and brick gallery. The Bronte Collection was loaned to the gallery, and the building opened in 1960. Soon miners with only a grade school education were seeing the works of Monet, Homer, Sisley, Renoir, Hassam, and Cassatt for the first time in their lives.

Elias died at 81 in 1962, and his bequest of a $500,000 endowment provided programmatic monies to operate the gallery. The gallery acquired additional paintings, and in 1965 purchased a major collection of works by Manet and

Cezanne. Most people credited the success of the gallery to the high-energy volunteer board of trustees who worked under the skillful guidance of Gallery Director Edwin "Bud" Hansen.

The Elias Bronte legacy has been carried on by Mary Bronte Leighton, who serves as board chair for the gallery. Mary's brother, Anthony Bronte, is also on the board, but he shows little interest in the gallery, frequently missing board meetings.

Prospective donors

In the words of many community leaders, Anthony Elias Bronte, 79, is "just like his old man"—hard-working and gruff, with a head for the mining business. But unlike his father, Tony doesn't seem interested in "putting back into the community." Whenever Tony has free time, he flies to his home in New York or to his villa in the south of France. He loves the life of the jet set. When Tony turned over the management of Great Virginia Mining to others, he and his wife Margaret began to spend even less time in Riverdale.

Mary Bronte left Riverdale to attend Cornell University and got her law degree from Columbia University. She began her career with a prestigious law firm in New York City where she eventually met Richard Leighton. Dick represented an MIT professor who claimed that his patent rights were violated by the industrial conglomerate that Mary represented. "I was attracted by Dick's concern for the underdog," she says. "To Dick, it was not just a case, it was a cause. He felt that basic principles of justice were being violated." Mary laughs, "I won the case, fell in love, and decided to return to Riverdale to practice general law for clients who needed representation more than the corporations I was used to representing."

Mary and Dick moved into the Bronte mansion. Within a few years, Mary was active on many of the same volunteer boards on which her father had served.

Bud Hansen summed up the general feelings of the Riverdale leaders who labeled Tony a "taker" and Mary a "giver." "Tony felt his contribution to community life was to keep the mine open in the recession-ridden seventies. He often said that "Jobs put more bread on the table than the high-minded Riverdale do-gooder volunteers."

Despite their differences in opinion and lifestyle, Tony and Mary remain close. Elias Bronte felt that "family came first," and brother and sister hold onto that ideal.

Development officer

Veronica Lassiter had an outstanding academic record in marketing at Syracuse University. After graduation, she was sought after by several firms. But she had married in college and now had small children, and she wanted a job that would enable her to balance her career responsibilities with her role as wife and mother. In 1978 she accepted a job as manager of the local Sears store because it meant she would not have to move from town to town.

She has been active on several volunteer boards, especially the PTA and

YMCA/YWCA. After much pressure from friends, she agreed to run for the Riverdale School Board. She was elected by a landslide and has served on the board for the past 12 years.

In 1985, the Riverdale Art Gallery Board decided to hire a full-time community relations and development officer to better organize fund-raising efforts. After drawing up the job specifications, one board member commented, "This describes Veronica Lassiter to a tee." The board asked her to consider leaving the retail business for the nonprofit world. After considerable soul-searching, she agreed. "Veronica took us out of the bake-sale mentality of fund raising," commented Bud Hansen. "We quit the tin-cup approach and professionalized the marketing of our needs." Veronica's skills in retailing and marketing have served her well in her new role. Giving has increased over 15 percent a year in the past seven years. Last year, annual giving totaled $1.5 million. In 1990, the gallery completed a special three-year appeal for $2.5 million to supplement the art acquisition fund.

Veronica is well-respected by the board of trustees, including Tony. He has commented, "Ronnie is tough, she knows this town, and she knows what it takes to succeed." Mary agrees. She considers Veronica a friend and confidante. "Veronica would have loved my dad. They share the same passion for art and the welfare of the Riverdale community," said Mary. "She is the glue that holds the gallery together."

Research background

At 76 Mary Bronte Leighton is a very wealthy woman. According to her father's probate filing, she was left the family estate, a selection of paintings, and many family heirlooms. The 1962 valuation, for estate tax purposes, was set at $12.8 million. According to county assessor records, the family estate is currently valued at $2.4 million. The 500-acre grounds behind the Bronte mansion contain the finest arboretum in the state.

In 1990, Mary donated a Mary Cassatt oil painting valued at $1.3 million. A painting by Jackson Pollack, valued at $750,000, was given on a permanent loan. Final transfer will take place at Mary's death.

Mary's income from her law practice averaged less than $50,000 a year, but Mary and Dick are shrewd investors. Mary told Veronica that the corporate merger mania of the 1980s had greatly benefited their portfolio. They sold securities valued at $3 million and established a family trust.

Anthony Elias Bronte has never known anything but wealth. His father left him stock in Great Virginia Mining valued at $12.5 million. Tony slowly sold shares of the publicly held corporation. Valuation of shares at time of sale exceed $20 million. According to the Great Virginia Mining corporate prospectus, Tony has 21,000 shares remaining. Current valuation of his holdings is $1.7 million.

Tony describes his townhouse in New York as "unpretentious" and his villa in France as "modest." Veronica has not visited either residence, but smiles at Tony's description. Tony spends a lot of money on himself. A home valued at $1.6 million, sports cars, and "the best suits Saville Row can make" give everyone the impression that Tony lives at the top edge of his earnings.

Mary and Tony give $150,000 each year to the gallery's annual fund. The gift is given in memory of their father. The size of the gift has not changed since 1985. Annual gifts from Mary and Tony total $2.1 million. In 1990, Tony donated $100,000 to the 1990 arts acquisition fund. Mary and Dick donated $250,000.

Major gift focus

After months of deliberation, the board of trustees decided that the decaying physical plant required their priority attention. Years of deferred maintenance have taken their toll. A report ordered by the board was compiled by a local engineering company. The estimated cost of repairs, refurbishment, and code-required changes totals $3.5 million.

The board ranked as a second priority the addition of 15,000 square feet to house the expanding collection. Research and restoration space would be included in this new area. The estimated cost is $1.8 million. Art conservation has been ignored in these plans because building repairs and additional space were considered a more important priority.

Veronica told the board that other public galleries were going to be more desirable locations for donated collections if the repairs and building addition were not completed in the near future. The board concurred heartily.

Assignment

You are Veronica Lassiter. You have been asked to present to the board a proposed fund-raising plan to raise sufficient funds to accomplish the $5.3 million goal for repair of the physical plant and construction of the gallery addition. As you begin to formulate your plan, you realize that the campaign cannot succeed without a lead gift of at least $2 million from Mary and Tony. Now consider the questions below.

Prepare your answers in writing. Then, if possible, discuss your strategy with a colleague who has also read the case and prepared written answers. Together turn to Section 3 and read the discussion of Case K, beginning on page 164.

1. Isn't the strategy very simple—just visit Mary and Tony and ask for the gift? What are your objectives?

2. What key areas of discussion will reveal information helpful to devising the requested plan?

3. What information needs to be obtained that isn't revealed in existing research?

4. How should you approach the question of gift focus?

5. How should the question of gift level be approached?

6. At this stage, how would you evaluate Riverdale Gallery's potential for obtaining a $2 million-plus gift from Tony and Mary?

Section 3:

Discussion of Case Studies

Alternatives and Possibilities

Y ou have read the case studies in Section 2 and answered the questions, based on your experience and background and what you have learned from this book. I encourage you to share your ideas and suggestions for solicitation strategies with a colleague who has also read the case studies and considered the questions. Because there is no "instruction manual" to successful major gift fund raising, the best way to learn how to do it is to do it. I hope that you were able to bring your own insights and experiences to bear on each of these case study situations as if it were a real-life problem, and you were the person responsible for solving it. I hope you have benefited from sharing your ideas with at least one other person. Now, read the discussion of each case study, but remember that this section is not meant to provide "the right answer," but only strategies and alternatives to help you think further into the situation.

Case A: James Knox College

1. Did you decide the overall strategy is flawed? A close bond exists between Deeble and Bob Rogers. Deeble is college president, Rogers is board chair. Eleven years of friendship between acknowledged peers exists. To send you, "the new boy," to explore gift focus and gift level seems to be a drastic error.

The reasoning behind this strategy, President Deeble says, is "to save me for the ask." Deeble is fearful that the discussion would be "inappropriate with me in attendance." The reasoning is understandable, but your chances of being successful seem slim.

Did you decide that both you and Deeble should go? What about including Abby?

2. Bob is clearly concerned about his future. Retirement is frightening. Why?

What is the story about Bob's son Steve and his reluctance to join the business? How well do the Rogers think Knox prepared Steve for a career?

What are the Rogers' attitudes about financial aid? Loans versus scholarships? Outside employment while attending school?

What are the Rogers' feelings about estate planning? How much of the family fortune should be left to the children?

What are the circumstances regarding Bob and Abby's meeting at Knox? Were the respective families happy with the choice of mates?

What role does sports play in a college education and at Knox? Were the Rogers active in sports?

The above questions will provide key points to developing an understanding of what Bob and Abby "see and hear" from their surroundings.

3. If gift level is a key point, it is crucial that both Bob and Abby Rogers be considered as prospects. Not just Bob! But unfortunately you know very little about Abby and her early history. What about the Whitey Award? What role did Abby play in the decision to make the gift in honor of her father? The key to gift size may rest on your knowledge of the quiet and shy Abby.

Do you need to know more about Katy and Steve? Professors may shed light on both of them. What are their personalities like? How are they alike? How are they different?

4. Did you agree that you should not meet with Bob Rogers by yourself? Should President Deeble be included? Should Abby be included? If your answer to these questions is "yes," your objectives might include:

• Learn more about Abby, Katy, and Steve Rogers.

• Explore the Rogers' feelings about the importance of undergraduate scholarships in providing a quality education to students who have financial need.

• Explore the Rogers' feelings about the Centennial Campaign and their role in it.

• Review the campaign plan, especially the gift table. Seek out Bob and Abby's opinion about the proposed gift table.

• Seek agreement for the preparation and presentation of a formal proposal regarding the Rogers' greatest area of interest.

5. At first, location of the meeting may seem to be a trivial matter. Bob is comfortable at the college or the Millvale Country Club. But Abby may be the deciding factor here. Perhaps President Deeble could suggest meeting at the Rogers' home. Abby may be most comfortable in her own surroundings and may enjoy acting as host.

Think carefully about research "holes." Perhaps the Rogers' home will provide clues to the some of the unanswered questions about Abby, Katy, and Steve.

6. You've already considered who should be included in the meeting. When all the facts are known, it will certainly appear that Abby is a key player and should be included. Deeble and the Rogers are peers. You are a facilitator.

7. How do the Rogers feel about their earlier gifts? Which gifts gave them the most satisfaction, then and now? Why?

Bob and Abby *may* have different levels of knowledge about the college's needs as well as gift opportunities. You should review these with them. Err on the side of repetition.

The board of trustees approved the needs listings. Were they correct?

8. At best, you and President Deeble will come out with a better feel for the appropriate gift range. Only an ask will confirm gift level.

Asking the above questions will serve as an excellent basis for narrowing the gift level.

Do you agree that, given the gift history, a multi-year pledge of $1 million seems initially feasible?

9. The last objective in Question 4 above ("Seek agreement for the preparation and presentation of a formal proposal...") is the key follow-up area. Now you need to ask if you may return with a leadership gift proposal. You should tie in the mention that the college also wants to discuss *their* (not his) volunteer leadership role in the campaign.

Would Abby consider a role separate from Bob's? Is there any harm in asking?

10. What do you think would happen if you followed the strategy discussed above? A four-year pledge of $250,000 per year certainly sounds appropriate given the information you have about this situation.

Case B: The Children's Alternatives Center

1. Did you decide that the advantages of meeting separately with Michael and with Susan outweighed any disadvantages? The disagreement is between brother and sister. Are they likely to divulge a lot of new information to you in a joint meeting?

Is the biggest disadvantage that the Noseks will talk to each other about their meetings? Is this a problem? If it is, how should it be overcome?

2. Isn't the biggest problem that you have very few facts, but myriad opinions? Doesn't Susan's remarks about their desire to make a gift need to be explored in depth? Do you know anything about their plans?

3. If you concentrate on determining gift focus, you will have walked by a number of unanswered questions. You must first seek information on their views of CAC's future, their role in the future, and their degree of devotion to their late father's vision. What type of gift is envisioned? What size? Is it one gift or two? Must Susan and Michael make a joint gift?

4. Susan and Michael are two people with individual strengths, strongly held views, and divergent views about their relationships to the CAC. A strategy involving a single approach may be filled with potential problems.

5. Do you have enough information to answer this question? The children of CAC's founder are wealthy and have a long record of service to the organization, but they seem to disagree on the future mission. Don't you need to know much more?

A leadership gift from Susan and Michael is critical to any major gift campaign effort. You are correct in considering this your top priority.

Case C: Lincoln State University

1. Did you decide a response to Elsie's letter was necessary? Should it be written or oral? What did Elsie reject, a gift or an interview for the feasibility study? Did you decide that this rejection is just another expression of Elsie's desire not to follow the conventional rules (as in her giving out $100 checks)?

2. Each of these people may be key to the focus and timing of the gift. Remember that Elsie has already told President Standard that "Lincoln Normal is in my will." Why did she tell Standard this? Was she hoping for a response that would clarify how he saw the mission of the university? You (Richelle)

have a close relationship with Elsie as well as an official role that makes you a very important person in the gift process. How can you work with the other people on this list to find out more about Elsie's intentions and interests?

3. Is any focus apparent? Has Elsie dealt with this issue in her will? How big a gift is she planning? Answers to these questions may well determine focus.

4. Are you ready for an orchestrated approach to Elsie? Shouldn't you concentrate instead on information-seeking from the cast of characters mentioned in Question 2?

5. Elsie loves Lincoln State University! Her involvement goes back almost 70 years. To her it is the same institution she knew in 1926, and she calls it by the same name, "Lincoln Normal College." Her life centers around the life of the institution. She has a strong motivation to give and the means to make a major gift. So the question is not whether she will give but when and how she will give. Elsie's view of the timing of the gift appears to differ from the university's view in which there is some sense of urgency if hers is to be a leadership gift in the campaign. The most important issue, then, centers on gift focus and whether Elsie can be persuaded of the benefit of making a substantial gift during her lifetime.

Case D: St. Mark's Children's Hospital

1. According to the information you have, Buzz Rice is a key to leadership in the campaign. He is a member of the hospital's governing board and has demonstrated philanthropic leadership through his recent pledge to double his annual gift. In short, Buzz Rice is a volunteer leader. His campaign gift may be another matter.

Buzz has demonstrated means to give a seven-figure gift. He has seen and approved the campaign plan and the gift table. His silence during consideration of the campaign cannot be taken as ignorance or lack of interest. He realizes that he will be expected to provide a significant lead gift. The question of gift level remains.

2. Researching an individual or private company has inherent limitations. Researching a person whose assets are in real estate is also limited. In this case, net asset value remains an open question that can be answered only by Buzz.

Additional data will be of marginal value. You have enough information to formulate a solicitation plan.

3. *The* primary objective is to get from Buzz a leadership gift of sufficient size to establish a benchmark for other prospective donors. In order to do that, Buzz will have to be convinced that he is the key to the campaign. The gift level is directly related to Buzz's understanding of his own importance to the success of the campaign.

A third objective involves the naming of the cancer care unit. Sister Mary Margaret is stepping down. Should the unit be named for her? Or perhaps naming should be conditioned on a gift of at least $3 million? Should this be the focus of the ask to Buzz Rice?

4. Perhaps the most important question is who should ask. Did you establish that you (Bill Goode) are the key? You weren't completely successful in your

last ask at a much lower level. There is no reason to believe that your relationship with Buzz goes beyond professional respect. But consider the relationship between Sister Mary and Buzz. Longtime friends. Policy-makers. Facility-builders. And Sister Mary is retiring. The cancer care unit is her farewell accomplishment. Professional respect is also evident in this relationship, but it is grounded on a solid peer relationship.

Three million dollars represents a "stretch" gift for Buzz. He will only consider this level when all the motivational factors for a major gift are present. It appears that Sister Mary is the only one who can bring out this level of motivation.

5. Buzz Rice understands finance and construction payout schedules. It may be possible to raise his gift sights by presenting him with a multiple-year gift proposal. What about a gift of $3 million payable over a three-year period?

Did you consider a matching challenge gift? Buzz could challenge certain board members by agreeing to match their contributions up to the $3 million ceiling. This proposal could be made if the board approves naming the building after Buzz.

6. The key to success is how much planning and attention you give to establishing your objectives and selecting your approach. There seems to be a high probability of securing a gift in excess of $1.5 million. The $3 million level depends on Sister Mary Margaret's ability to tie the success of the project to Buzz Rice's decision about the level of the gift.

Did you consider Buzz's health in making your prediction of success? Is Buzz's realization of his own mortality a positive or negative factor in his decision to make a gift?

Case E: Kamps for Kids/Nature Outreach

1. Your first move should be to step back from the situation and evaluate it in a dispassionate manner. Such analysis is often difficult when you are focusing on the donation rather than the donor.

What is the status of ongoing cultivation? Do you need to start all over again? Are the earlier efforts of John Rodee a factor to consider? Is the establishment of a Thomas family foundation a factor that should be considered? It certainly changes the gift decision-making process.

2. All indications are that decisions regarding philanthropy are deferred to Edgar. But Ruth and Laurel have separate interests and are active in other areas. The extent of Edgar's role needs to be checked out carefully. He *is* a major factor, but how much of a factor?

Ruth is a civic and voluntary leader in the community. Although she downplays her role, the original decision to donate the land was not made by Edgar alone, but by Edgar and Ruth together. What is the extent of her influence?

Laurel is the pride of her father and his eventual successor as CEO of Thomas Supermarkets. She is a major player *now* and in the future. You need to consider her role in present and, especially, future gift decisions. Downplaying Laurel's role would be a grave mistake.

Did you think about the three other Thomas children? Their roles haven't been considered, but they may well be significant factors in decisions about the family foundation.

3. Your friendship with the Thomases predates your role with Nature Outreach. You were not aware of the Thomas connection when you took the job. The Thomases know this. They are also aware that, to date, you have not let your professional role interfere with your friendship.

Certainly your deep insight into the family is a plus. No one at Nature Outreach has this dual concern for the organization and the Thomas family. Your passion for the organization is known and understood. At one point— before you met them—Edgar and Ruth Thomas shared this passion. As long as you treat your friendship and your job as intertwined but separate, you should be able to enjoy both successfully.

4. The board expects results. Priority needs have been established. You want to meet those needs. You are goal-oriented. Given these realities, you may be tempted to establish soliciting a gift as your primary objective. But is this a realistic first step? Wouldn't it be better to concentrate on reestablishing the link between Nature Outreach and Edgar and Ruth Thomas?

The Thomases *are* linked to Kamps for Kids—whether they like it or not. Although they are neighbors, a psychological fence has been built, and it's a high one. Edgar wants nothing to do with "those damn tree huggers." Shouldn't you establish as your first objective a lowering of this fence?

5. Only two possibilities exist—you and John Rodee. John is the connection to the past. You are the connection to the present. Both of you are concerned about the future of Nature Outreach. Each of you can play a key role in solicitations.

Remember that Edgar gave you an opening when he mentioned his idea for a demonstration farm. Edgar doesn't make idle remarks. What should you do? Approach Edgar and ask if he would like to discuss his idea and get reacquainted with the organization? How about discussing Edgar's remark with Laurel and asking her advice about how to follow up?

Location for a visit may be an important consideration. Should you meet in Edgar's office? This would downplay your social relationship and, until the Thomases indicate differently, you should follow standard protocol when you are discussing business. Once you have gotten a green light from Laurel about following up on Edgar's remark, your request to Edgar to meet with you and John Rodee is likely to be met with a positive response.

6. Gift focus is really not important at this point, but don't lose sight of the organization's list of priority needs. Edgar's remark regarding a demonstration farm may or may not indicate a deeply felt need or a well-thought-out idea. Perhaps he was simply expressing his regret for the loss of a former close association in which he has a significant investment. Your conversation with Laurel should have given you some insight on this point.

Once you have reestablished the connection between Edgar and Nature Outreach, you can explore ways in which his idea of setting up an old-fashioned farm can support the organization's new priorities—such as, for example, the goal of establishing a working tree farm.

Are Nature Outreach's new priorities all ideas for the '90s? Or are they traditional ideas dressed up in modern language? Could both agendas be reviewed for similarities? Is a win/win situation possible? Could a demonstration farm encompass the current identified needs? Is matching the organization's priorities with the Thomases' needs an important issue to consider?

7. Gift level is a very low consideration at this point. The Thomas family has the capacity to give a major gift. Edgar mentioned land, not money. At this point, shouldn't you stick with ideas and worry later about the cost of bringing the ideas to reality?

8. The selection of priorities and the process you follow are the keys to success. If the strategy follows from a thoughtful evaluation of the facts, your chances of obtaining a significant gift appear to be quite good.

Timing is a critical factor. The Thomas family does not make snap decisions regarding philanthropy. Can you be bold enough to tell the major gift committee that a longer-range strategy is needed?

Case F: Weston Symphony

1. Is this the time to think small and assume limited objectives? Perhaps. To date, there has been no dialogue with E.B. at all. Her comments on the symphony audience have received no response of any kind from the organization. As far as E.B. is concerned, she hasn't been heard, and her concerns are not shared by anyone else.

Isn't your major objective to meet with E.B, hear her out, and acknowledge her concerns? It is almost impossible to establish other objectives until an airing of her concerns has taken place.

A second objective would be to thank E.B. for her continued support and attendance. Like everyone else, she likes to be appreciated. Regardless of level, her efforts shouldn't go unnoticed.

2. E.B. is a mover and shaker in the academic, medical, and literary worlds. She is bright and approachable. A third-person go-between seems unnecessary. A telephone call for an appointment with a confirming letter seems like the right thing to do.

See Question 6 below regarding who else should be included in this meeting.

3. E.B. has defined the first topic of discussion—her concerns over audience makeup. She isn't aware of the board's similar concern. E.B. is concerned with the type of person who fills the seat. The board is concerned with filling the seat. Is there enough common concern for a discussion on this issue?

Does a third area of programming—one that will attract a more diverse audience—suggest itself? What have other symphonies and orchestras done in this area? Should you be prepared with this information?

By the end of the discussion, E.B. will at least feel that she has been heard *if* you have stayed with your objective to listen and to gather information. The temptation to justify and explain the current situation may be very strong. But it's important to avoid doing too much of the talking. In this case, your responsive silence may be the best thing you can say because it says, "I hear you."

4. E.B. is a passionate advocate for causes that are not your top priority. Your college experiences were very different. It is very easy to dwell on the differences, but what are the interests? The first is love of good music. The second is support for the Weston Symphony. This is a safe area to share

similarities and differences.

You can only respect E.B.'s opinions if you understand them. You are not meeting to compare ideologies. Your job is not to convert her to your views, but to listen to her concerns and explore remedies.

E.B. will respect you—although she will probably never embrace your political views—when she sees how well you listen and how genuinely you try to understand how she feels.

5. As a meeting site, the office at the medical center has limited appeal. As "Dr. Jackson" E.B. will be more concerned with her patients' problems than with yours. At best, you'll be "squeezed in," and most likely squeezed out.

Her private practice office has similar deficiencies. E.B. sees a different patient every 20 minutes. She has an obligation to her partners to carry her share of the patient load. Avoid this location.

Your first objective is to get acquainted. Her personal office is in her townhouse, so she may not wish to meet you there. Is breakfast, lunch, or dinner a possibility? How about dinner before the next concert? She will be in town and can probably calendar this time more easily than other times.

6. E.B. first expressed her views to several board members. Do you think one of those board members should be included in your meeting? What criterion would you use in selecting a board member? Does being a good listener seem to be the most important criterion?

Does gender of the board member appear to be important? Would a woman board member enhance the potential of meeting your objectives? How about political views as a criterion? On the other hand, might two people who agree on social policy drift away from the needs of the Weston Symphony?

7 and 8. The board has established the priorities of need. But E.B. is expressing a problem. So far, no discussion of solutions has been held. A solution will suggest focus. The nature of the solution will suggest gift level.

For example, perhaps your discussion focuses on bringing inner-city middle school students to the pops series held each spring. You and E.B. decide that 100 students per concert is a worthwhile goal. You can "cost out" the idea and then discuss E.B.'s willingness to share in the effort. The first priority is to understand the concern. The second priority is to seek solutions. Specific ideas contain price-tags to bring them to reality.

Your goal is to relax and let the information-seeking take place. If this occurs, the rest of the process will naturally follow.

9. It is highly unlikely that a first meeting that focuses on listening will result in agreement on a gift. But the discussion will focus on various solutions that will require research on your part. Answers to this research will form the basis for a follow-up meeting.

Might it be worthwhile to invite E.B. to express her concerns directly to the board? This idea undermines your assignment from the board, but it may be a positive move. If you consider this option carefully, think of the possible risks.

Does a pilot project sound feasible? Underwriting a one-time experiment would get E.B. involved. She could easily get excited with positive outcomes that suggest a much bigger program.

10. It's impossible to guess the potential of a major gift at any level above the mid-five figures. The process will ascertain whether she can be motivated to give. The means to make a major gift appear to exist. The support is there.

Motivating E.B. to decide to take ownership of the project is your job.

Case G: Jamesfield Academy

1. If you can avoid the first major danger area, you have a relatively clear road ahead. Esther has called and said, "I'm interested in your views." Is that the objective? Does the long-term friendship and weekly meetings mean you should ignore the communication funnel? Should you go directly to information-giving?

No! Esther Johnson is a woman of strong opinions. She has opinions on gift timing, gift focus, and gift level, but you don't know what they are. You should come prepared with the facts from the planning study. The board set the priorities and Esther concurred. But how did she feel about the report? Her vote was recorded; her actions were not.

Why did she speak against William's motion to conduct a feasibility study? Is this another objective—to discover her thinking on this issue?

How do the other family members feel about these issues? Does this suggest another objective?

2. Esther understands philanthropy and the campaign process. She is a one-person donor screening committee. Her views on a future campaign might reveal a lot about her gift level intentions at this time.

What are Esther's views on campaign leadership? What role would she assume? How about Charlotte, William, and J.J.? What would their roles be? How does Esther feel about Donald Barbour's role? If Esther were you, how would she proceed, short-term and long-term? Role reversal might reveal a lot of information.

3. Gifts from the Johnson Family Trust are recorded and revealed publicly. Is a multimillion dollar gift from the Trust possible? What are the gift level restrictions, if any? Do family members make gifts outside the trust? What are the extent of these personal gifts? Remember the scholarship!

It is imperative that you know the rules of the Trust and the personal giving habits of family members outside the Trust. Public records will reveal the details of the Family Trust, since it is held as a public foundation. Discovering the giving habits of the family members is a greater challenge. You have a close relationship with Esther. She said, "I'll be interested in your views." Isn't it fair to ask her to clarify her statement? Did she mean she is considering something through the Trust or on her own? Open-ended questions and aggressive listening are imperative here.

4. As we have discussed, if you do some aggressive listening, Esther will probably reveal her thoughts on gift focus. Perhaps the academy's needs are so great that Esther is overwhelmed. If so, then she needs to explore the pros and cons of each project—not from your view but from hers. You may wish to suggest additional benefits of each project to the institution, but Esther needs to stay in the lead.

At some point, other family members' views become important, but not until Esther's views are considered. You must be careful not to play one family member off against the other. With Esther's permission, perhaps you could suggest a further joint discussion with Charlotte. William wants to move forward with a capital campaign feasibility study. He'll volunteer his views freely at that time.

Did you consider a family challenge gift? How about a combination of projects? Would a grouping of projects raise the Johnsons' gift level sights and bring about consensus? Is a multi-year gift in order?

5. Gift level will flow from an identification of the need and the ownership of the solution to that need. Esther has had 80 years of history with Jamesfield. She has surely given thought to named gifts. Elmer did not, in her view, receive proper tribute with the naming of the quad. What would be appropriate? Does she have a view on that?

Esther mentioned that she grows older each day. Does that suggest she is considering what Cornell University's David Dunlop calls an "ultimate gift"?

6. Your prospects for a major gift are excellent. As always, the process of reaching the goal is in your hands. You must carefully orchestrate it one step at a time and keep your objectives in front of you as you move forward.

Case H: Huntington University

1. Two donors with significant major gift potential are about to be told that the institution does not value their views on global peace and conflict resolution. As we know, institutionalization of personal views is an important motivation to make a major gift.

The Bolands will not care about the problems their gift brings to Huntington University. The sting of rejection will transcend reason. The embarrassment of being turned down publicly will affect their relationship with Huntington for many years. It may even sever that relationship. Perhaps if either Tom or Susan were a member of the board of trustees, they would understand the problems, but their "outsider" status heightens the seriousness of the situation.

2. Sarah Bromfield has a lot riding on the successful resolution of this situation. Personally, she is close to the Bolands and will be embarrassed if they are alienated. Professionally, she is in a delicate position. She approved the direct approach to the board of trustees that gave rise to the problem. In short, this problem is the president's. Thus, your first objective is defined: to solve the problem without alienating the Bolands.

The president needs to hear that "we"—that is you and she—have a problem that requires a joint solution.

3. Isn't acceptance or rejection of the gift the least of your concerns? If you recommend accepting the gift, you must plan how to solve the financial and academic problems. Rejection of the gift without a contingency plan accomplishes nothing.

Let's review the problems. The institution is substantially reducing its budget. Tuition increases are pegged to inflation. The faculty will not be willing to add a program when existing programs are being cut back. The terms of the gift, $100,000 each year for five years, means that the chair couldn't be filled for six years. The gift is less than half of a full chair endowment, and support costs haven't been considered.

If you hold to the communication funnel, then your first objective is information-seeking. Do you really know what the Bolands envision with their gift? Your only insight was a very brief statement to the board. Don't you need to know more? Perhaps the problem isn't as great as first appeared.

Perhaps your first advice to President Bromfield is that she visit with the Bolands to "discuss their generous gift and the challenge to their alma mater to move forward in this new area of inquiry, peace and conflict resolution." She should listen to what they hope the gift will accomplish. Did they mean an academic chair? Do they know what a chair entails? Are there other ways to accomplish their goals?

If President Bromfield visits the Bolands, what options does she have in responding to their challenge? Let's consider some options of how the endowment earnings might be spent:

• Create a Boland Professorship to study the economics of peace or the politics of peace. This option could utilize existing faculty or add faculty in existing departments.

• Create a Boland Lecture Series, an annual lecture series focusing on the resolution of conflict by peaceful means. The Bolands could co-chair a committee to work with faculty in inviting distinguished speakers from around the world.

• Create a Boland Fellowship to allow a graduate student to do research on various aspects of peace. The findings could be published and presented in a public lecture.

• Establish a committee composed of the Bolands, President Bromfield, faculty members, distinguished alumni, and trustees to outline uses for the gift. As the endowment earnings increase, additional components of the Boland Center for Peace could be activated. The advantage of this option is that the committee would be charged with how best to use this generous gift.

The key to success is President Bromfield's ability to listen to the Bolands. Perhaps some of the above ideas are already options considered by the Bolands. Their ideas could be used rather than those proposed by Sarah Bromfield.

4. By all means, set a meeting with the Bolands immediately. President Bromfield should phone Susan or Tom and request a get-together as soon as possible.

5. The major objective of the meeting is to listen to the Bolands to see what the university can do to help turn their dreams into reality. The areas for possible compromise are numerous. The Bolands are bright. Converting ideas into action is their way of life.

Propose options only after you are confident that they are congruent with the Bolands' thinking.

6. You were classmates with Susan and Tom; they see you as a key staff member. Sarah Bromfield is the leader of the institution; the Bolands see her as their friend and their peer. You can staff the president and handle all the details of implementing the gift.

7. Holding the meeting in President Bromfield's office sends one message. Holding it in her home sends another one. The same is true for Tom's or Susan's office or their home. Since President Bromfield is proposing the meeting, she could say, "I'd love to have you out to the university. We could meet in my office for a while and walk over to the house for lunch." Another option is to make the above suggestions and then add, "If it's more convenient to meet somewhere else, I'm open to that. It's important that we act on your generous gift as quickly as possible." This follow-up comment establishes that the president sees the gift as an important institutional priority.

8. Establishing gift focus is the central objective. As far as the Bolands are

concerned, gift focus is already set. The question remains how to implement their intentions in a way that is compatible with the university's needs. Aggressive listening and a problem-solving attitude will lead to the answers.

9. You must address gift level. The mechanics of how an academic chair is established, when it is funded, and how recruiting takes place are rarely understood by prospective donors. As the Bolands come to understand these realities, they may opt to increase their gift or to accelerate the timing of payments. These options will arise out of the discussion that follows an understanding of what the Bolands hope to accomplish.

10. The Bolands care passionately about the goal of solving global conflict by peaceful means. Huntington University can implement their dream and add the prestige of the institution to their advocacy. Both parties have mutually compatible needs. The solution lies in following a process that brings the win/ win options to the forefront.

The chances for a gift in excess of $500,000 are excellent. Your view of the situation needs a larger lens. The Bolands are beginning philanthropists. Your job is to make the experience enjoyable so it is repeated throughout their lifetimes.

Case I: The Center for Gender Studies

1. Ann invited you to share the panel's report when it was completed, so she, in essence, has set the agenda for the meeting. If the board of governors has already adopted the report, then Ann's opinions are relatively unimportant— except as they relate to the exploration of possible gift areas in future meetings.

Ann likes to give opinions, and she is knowledgeable about each of the recommended program areas. She needs to be heard in the widest forum and at the highest levels. Since Ann was invited by the board to serve on the panel, she could be requested to file an official commentary that the board could adopt and append to the report. The lay panel members are Ann's "dear friends." They need her friendship in their professional pursuits. They would likely welcome her input.

Your first objective is to get Ann's opinions officially recognized as important and worthy of consideration.

A second important objective is to persuade Ann to give serious consideration to leading the campaign as chair. She has the experience as a volunteer leader and the interest to be concerned about the campaign's success. You have two major hurdles to overcome: She has never been asked to give a major gift to the center, and you are her only connection to the center.

2. The long-term objective is to move Ann into a stable leadership role. She contributes generous annual gifts in relation to other supporters, but she is still an "outsider." She has never been to a board of governors meeting; she has never been asked to be a member of the board; and she has never served the center in an official capacity.

3. Don't confuse *quantity* of research with *quality*. Most of the press clippings are based on rumors. Ann heads a private company that is not required to publicly divulge its worth.

Ann loves to talk, but is not forthcoming about her own wealth. All indications are that she has a lot of money, spends a lot of money, gives a lot of money to causes she believes in, and raises a lot of money from others to support these causes. But do you have any hard data that demonstrate her willingness to give a significant campaign leadership gift? She has the capacity to make a $1 million gift, but research on her willingness to do so is limited.

4. Ann is comfortable both in her office and in her condominium. She can determine the location of the meeting. The office location would put her in a business frame of mind so that she might review the report as she reviews so many reports each working day. You would be competing with the heavy demands of running a major corporation.

Meeting in Ann's home offers the advantage of a more relaxed atmosphere and more in keeping with your objective of getting her to donate a significant part of her "volunteer time" to the center as campaign chair. Ann is likely to give stronger consideration to your request if it is made out of the office.

5. Ann likes you, but you and she are not peers. Scholars from the center provide interesting conversation which Ann thoroughly enjoys but, again, they are not peers. Volunteering is often done without selfish motivation, but the experience is enhanced when the volunteer is put in contact with important peers. Volunteering can confer status and recognition. As development officer, it is your job to assist in the process.

Members of the board of governors can help, and perhaps they should be introduced to Ann so that she can establish relationships with other people who care about the center's mission. The lay panel members could prove helpful. What does Ann think of the mayor? The senator? The union head? Would it be helpful to have one of them attend the meeting to hear Ann's opinions of the report?

6. Gift focus is a matter for Ann to decide and define. She is connected by profession and passion to each of the program areas. Each program has certain psychic benefits. It is your job to discover how Ann balances the scales and with which program (or programs) she most closely identifies.

Be forewarned: Ann will have her own ideas about how these priority programs should be implemented. If she is to give volunteer leadership and a major gift, the center must be prepared to hear and consider her ideas.

7. Gift level is a third-level consideration. First, you need to secure Ann's agreement to chair the campaign. Second, you have to discover how she identifies with the program priorities. Each of the programs as she envisions them has a price-tag associated with it. Thus, gift level is determined by Step 2 and shaped by Step 1. Vision to accomplish a goal will ultimately determine the gift level.

8. The approach will determine the outcome. If Ann can be convinced by peers that her leadership will make a significant difference, then the prospect is very high. If, on the other hand, you ignore the peer process and appeal only to her sense of duty, your prospects for success are much lower.

9. The Silverman Center for the Study of Gender and Politics? An approach by the senator and the mayor?

The Silverman Center for the Study of Gender and Industry? An approach by the mayor and the head of the union?

If either of these "fit" Ann's vision of her role in a national concern for gender studies, your prospects for obtaining a leadership gift above $2.5 million are enhanced.

Perhaps leadership (campaign chair) comes first and the gift approach should be made in the closing stages of the nucleus phase of the campaign. But you will be severely hampered by the failure to ask for a major gift in the years preceding the campaign.

Will Ann Silverman move from annual gift to major gift? Yes. When? The answer is less clear. As Woody Allen said once, 80 percent of success is just showing up.

Case J: University Hospital

1. Martin and Karen Walters disagree about the priority of needs for the hospital, but at no time have they expressed a lack of enthusiasm. Their emotional support of University Hospital remains strong. But their disagreement presents a challenge. What is the basis of the disagreement? Why does Martin favor buildings over research? Why does Karen focus on research? Your first objective is to explore these questions.

Do you need to have agreement between Martin and Karen in order to obtain a major gift or gifts? What is the Walters' larger giving pattern beyond University Hospital and the Ronald McDonald House? Should this question be considered in determining your second objective?

Gift capacity is a major question. There are 71 projects in the long-range plan. The philanthropic opportunities range from $100,000 (equipment and research fellowships) to $3.5 million (expansion of patient bed capacity). But you have very little research to guide you to conclusions about gift level. Learning more about the Walters' gift level capacity should be considered as a third objective, but only after you have completed the first two objectives.

2. Perhaps the Walters are too close to the trees (that is they may be seeing only the 71 gift opportunities) to see the forest. You need to help them step back and consider the larger picture. You are dealing with major donors who care about the future of University Hospital. What is their long-term, larger vision of the future? Where do they want the hospital to direct its energies in the next 10 years? This "vision thing" needs exploration.

Martin will not continue his 18-hour day work pattern forever. How does he see his own future? What passions will receive his priority attention then? Karen, too, cannot continue indefinitely to put all her energies into fundraising efforts for the parents' support group. How does she see her own life in the next five to 10 years?

3. The research appears complete. Large gifts and large giving capacity are demonstrated. But you know very little about the Walters Group and the exact nature of Martin and Karen's ownership. Is consideration of a planned gift your major priority? This area needs more research.

The Walters have three other children besides Debbie. How do these children fit into the future plans for the family? How might the other children be a positive or negative influence on any major gift?

The missing research cannot come from formal sources. The Walters themselves must be the source. Future strategies must include obtaining additional research in the above-mentioned areas.

4. Did you consider meeting with the Walters separately? This would avoid putting either one in the position of having to defend his or her preferences against the other. At all costs, you must avoid playing off one against the other. Your focus is to listen and understand rather than to mediate a disagreement.

If you feel separate meetings are important, then the scheduling and conduct of the meeting are critical. Perhaps you could suggest that certain individuals in separate focus groups be interviewed further. Then separate meetings are required and seem natural. Your job is to recommend a major gift strategy that best facilitates a major gift or gifts of the donors' own choosing.

During the actual meetings, you should focus on the individual feelings and opinions rather than conflict. At all times, remember that Debbie is the reason for their concern for these issues and their support of the hospital.

5. There is a large cast to consider—yourself, Dean Huetter, Director Lee, and Dr. Muncie. Each has a specific role in the functioning of the hospital. Each has specific contributions and information.

Dr. Muncie seems to have a key role. As Karen has said, he is working toward a "cure for this dreaded illness." Muncie remains the link between Debbie and the Walters.

Huetter and Lee represent the administration. Their views of priorities are very important in the long-range plan for the hospital. They need to be involved.

You are the catalyst among these people; you are the one who will make things happen. Your job is to understand the contribution of each person and recommend a continued cultivation and solicitation strategy.

In the initial meetings, Huetter and Lee can concentrate on getting the Walters' view of the "big picture." All the priorities can be discussed, ranked, or discarded. Consider Huetter and Lee for the first meetings.

Once it has been determined that the Walters' primary concern remains mental health, then Dr. Muncie becomes the key player. He is the one to weave emotion and vision into a gift proposal. He can best describe the cost and the benefit of specific gift ideas.

Your role is to facilitate each meeting and act as staff liaison/recorder. You are the director of each step. You are the person who is responsible for getting consensus on what you, Huetter, Lee, and Muncie saw and heard. Aggressive listeners can disagree on what they have heard, and it's up to you to make sure that unwarranted inferences do not occur.

6. Gift focus is the first central question. Your objectives deal with understanding gift focus. But in this situation you are not trying to guide donors toward a predetermined need. You already have a big menu of needs. Your goal is to discover which need ignites passion and excites the donors to action. Your goal is to listen and to discover the focus of the Walters' interests. And they will tell you if you remain in the information-seeking mode. Can you relax and let the process occur?

7. Gift level is your second central concern. Capacity, in this case, will be a function of gift focus. Vision will dictate gift level.

Perhaps Martin and Karen will never agree on a specific gift area. You should avoid a conflict that results in no action at all. In this case, your strategy should be to consider the possibility of presenting two proposals for the Walters' consideration. But the prospects for success would be considerably greater if you could present a proposal that was agreeable to both of them. For example, a proposal that adds space (such as research laboratories) and staff (such as research fellows) could be combined into a single proposal. Many other combinations are possible once you understand the underlying motivations of the donors.

8. The chances of a gift in excess of $1 million are excellent. But is that amount a measure of success? An ultimate gift should be your focus here. Once you get to know these donors better, you will be able to find the gift area that will raise their gift sights considerably. Don't settle for a short-term strategy that results in a significantly smaller gift.

Case K: Riverdale Art Gallery

1. At first glance, the case seems simple: Tony will give a gift if asked. Mary will certainly give a gift if asked. You could return to the board with a plan that indicates a slight upgrade in giving for all previous donors. Quick mathematics reveal the challenge that such a plan would present.

In 1980 the gallery completed a $2.5 million campaign. It took three years of hard work, and many of the donors "stretched" to reach this target. Now you are considering a goal more than twice as big.

Clearly, you have to prepare a campaign plan that contains a realistic gift table. Tony Bronte and Mary Bronte Leighton will be at the top of the table as they have been for the past 40 years. But how do you get Tony and Mary to stretch their own sights to consider a $2 million-plus gift?

Your first objective is to prepare a campaign case statement that is compelling enough to allow Tony and Mary to see a larger vision. This campaign, unlike the first, is not about art acquisition. Rather it is focused on "the house that Elias built." Their father's vision included building that house. That vision was a part of his ultimate gift. Now the house is falling apart.

Elias put his art collection in the gallery as an incentive for others to follow suit. But today there is not enough room to properly display and expand the collection. Elias's dream is in jeopardy. Tony and Mary have to see and understand that the Bronte family torch was passed to them. They now must consider their final gift the same way their father did over 30 years ago.

2. All discussions with Tony and Mary in the past have been on present-day concerns. Annual funds and collection expansion are short-term matters. You don't know how they feel about the future of the gallery after their deaths. You need this information, but it can only come from Mary and Tony.

What provisions have Mary and Tony already made for the gallery in their wills? This information is the key to understanding their feelings about the present plans. Both are members of the board; they both approved the plan. It is time to move from guessing and hoping about their estate plans.

3. The key area of research that is missing concerns the estate plans of Tony and Mary. Many small organizations, such as the Riverdale Art Gallery, fail to deal with the after-life plans of their founding benefactor family. You cannot afford to make that mistake in this case.

You know that Tony makes a lot of money and spends a lot of money. Gossip is that he lives on the economic edge. But is this true? Does he have the capacity for such a large gift? This question of gift capacity needs to be explored.

Complacency is evident in the research of Bronte heirs. The gallery has always assumed that it knows them well. They are family. But in order to develop a sound strategy, you need to know more.

4. You (Veronica) are the person at center stage. Tony admires you; Mary considers you a friend and confidante. But timing is the key. You should not approach the task of writing the case statement without exploring it with the members of the board. You need to sit down with Tony and Mary and explore whether they agree that this campaign is the turning point in keeping their father's dream alive.

Mary and Tony have to write the case statement themselves, with you functioning as a listening ear. Compelling words have to come from them. No one else can spell out how the Bronte legacy will continue—or end—except the authors themselves. Once they have helped write the statement of need, they will own it, and it will be up to them to sell it to the rest of the board and to the community.

This does not seem to be the right time to sell "half a loaf." Both the repairs and the addition are part of the dream. Staging the project should only be considered as a last resort. In short, the focus is to complete both projects.

Art conservation is a critical part of the mission of the Riverdale Art Gallery. Both Tony and Mary own highly valued art. You need to convince them that if they give works of art from their own collections, the pieces will be properly cared for. At this stage, you are not focusing on this issue, but you cannot ignore it as an important long-term concern. The first issue in art conservation is to properly house and display the art. That is your focus.

5. Is now the time to consider naming the new building "The Bronte Gallery of Riverdale"? Although Elias Bronte refused to have his name on the original building, memorializing oneself or a loved one is the strongest motivation in major gift-giving. Can you afford to ignore this issue? Should you discreetly consult the other board members before approaching Tony and Mary about the issue?

What is your opinion? Should the contributions over three lifetimes of Brontes be honored in this way?

First, you should meet with Tony and Mary to secure their help in writing the case statement. After reaching agreement on a compelling statement, you should seek their concurrence about the name change. The third step should be to return to Mary and Tony with a plan that shows the refurbished building and the addition with the new name on the front.

At this point, you need to stress that you are conveying the wishes of the board when you ask Tony and Mary to consider the name change in honor of their considering a $2 million gift.

6. The odds of your success in obtaining a $2 million-plus gift depend on the outcome of your research, the donors' participation in the writing of the statement of need, and their concurrence regarding the name change. If these steps are successful, you will be successful.

About the Author

Richard E. Matheny

Richard E. Matheny is widely known in higher education circles throughout the United States and internationally as a speaker, writer, and consultant. He has served as a consultant in fund raising, management, and communications strategies for more than 100 colleges and universities.

Following a successful career in real estate administration and association management, Rich became executive vice president of the Whitworth College Foundation in 1977. In 1980, Rich was named vice president of Whitworth College in Spokane, Washington. He left Whitworth in early 1985 to assume the position of vice chancellor and chief development officer at the University of California, Irvine (UCI).

His educational background includes a bachelor's degree from Washington State University, a master's degree from the University of Southern California, and a doctorate in Educational Leadership from Gonzaga University. He has written numerous articles on management and communication. In 1982, he authored *Creating Charitable Trusts in Real Estate*, which has became a standard reference book in the planned giving field. In 1988, Rich was appointed vice chancellor for university relations at the University of California, Davis. This position involves the management of six departments and a $7 million budget.

In January 1989, Rich received the CASE District VII Tribute Award for Professional Achievement. In December 1992, he received the Outstanding Fund-Raising Executive Award from NSFRE Capital Chapter, Sacramento, California. In June 1994, Rich received the "Steuben Apple" award from CASE for excellence in teaching.

During 1991, Matheny was a Fulbright Fellow in the United Kingdom.

NOTES

NOTES

NOTES